A TASTE FOR SPEED

Also by John Joseph Kelly:

Roostertail: The Miss Supertest Story. (Lincoln, Nebraska: iUniverse Inc., 2008), 211 pp.

A TASTE FOR SPEED
THE BIOGRAPHY OF WILL BRADEN:
CANADA'S TOP RACEBOAT DRIVER 1915-1958

JOHN JOSEPH KELLY

iUniverse, Inc.
New York   Bloomington

A Taste for Speed
The Biography of Will Braden: Canada's Top Raceboat Driver 1915-1958

iUniverse books may be ordered through booksellers or by contacting:

iUniverse
1663 Liberty Drive
Bloomington, IN 47403
www.iuniverse.com
1-800-Authors (1-800-288-4677)

Because of the dynamic nature of the Internet, any Web addresses or links contained in this book may have changed since publication and may no longer be valid. The views expressed in this work are solely those of the author and do not necessarily reflect the views of the publisher, and the publisher hereby disclaims any responsibility for them.

ISBN: 978-1-4502-4789-4 (sc)
ISBN: 978-1-4502-4790-0 (ebk)

Printed in the United States of America

iUniverse rev. date: 08/30/2010

In memory of my mother, Florence Laura Kelly (1929-2009) who inspired me by her constant perseverance and courage in the face of ill health throughout her life. I miss you Mom!

"He was the kind of guy who would sit up all night and help you fix your boat so you could beat him in the races the next day"

Preface and Acknowledgements

There were times when I was researching this manuscript that I felt I **knew** Bill Braden. This was because I had come across an anecdotal story from a family member or a friend which filled in a detail that was important to the mental image I had created of the man. More often than not, I felt I knew him because I had looked into his eyes in the hundreds of photos he took that have survived a half century beyond him: the movie star good looks, the athlete, the veteran of World War II, the fact that he was Canada's top race boat driver over a twelve year period, the loving father who would attend his children's school athletic events.

The most difficult part of writing the biography of a man who has been dead for over a half century is that Mr. Braden did not leave behind a daily diary, nor a sheaf of correspondence with individuals about his racing career, or even correspondence with his wife. So the author has no idea what Mr. Braden was thinking/feeling about his racing career, or about life in general. Nor have his papers from his years at the Hamilton Street Railway survived.

This book could not have been written without the assistance and support of Will Braden's children. Let me start with Bill Braden Jr., who has been a friend for almost fifteen years. Bill helped me with materials about his father when I was writing my previous book on the history of **Miss Supertest.** Those materials formed the basis for my desire to write a biography of Will Braden because he sounded like such an interesting guy, and he lived such a fascinating life. Second son, John Braden was good enough to share with me photos, personal correspondence with his Dad, and information over the phone. Third son, Norm, was kind enough to share anecdotal stories about his Dad. Gwyn, the sole daughter in the family, hosted a lunch where I got to meet all of the Bradens, and hear them reminisce about growing up around Will Braden. Gwyn shared with me photo albums and scrapbooks her father kept during the war that were in her possession. Dave Braden arranged several interviews in the Hamilton area, and also shared the photo album of his Dad's 1935 motorcycle trip across Europe. I also appreciate the hospitality Dave and Cathy showed me when I dropped by their house one day to talk about Will Braden. Finally, Mike

Braden, the youngest in the family, arranged an interview for me with Bob Hutcheson, who was present at Fairy Lake on that fateful day in August 1958. My thanks to each and every one of them. My hope is that they will be pleased with this finished product, and the story it tells; and they will feel that the trust they had in me to chronicle their father's life was justified.

People were willing to answer questions and send materials through the mail to assist the author in his research. Viola Lyons, Assistant Archivist at the J.D. Burns Archives at Trinity College School, sent along Bill's school records from his years at T.C.S. (1929-1933), as well as copies of the School Record whenever Bill appeared in it, since he was an athlete of some repute on campus. Barbara Stromstad of the Alumni Department at Le Rosey in Switzerland, forwarded Bill's academic scores from the school, along with copies of the Echo de Rosey, which once again illustrated Bill's athletic prowess.

John Russo, from the ATIP and Personnel Records Service Branch at the Archives of Canada was good enough to find and copy Bill Braden's military personnel file from World War II, and fill in this crucial gap from his life. Cindy Slinn, the Marketing Co-Coordinator in the Transit Division, of the Public Works Department of the City of Hamilton, was good enough to give me access to and guide me through the papers of the Hamilton Street Railway, and allow me to see the working world that Bill was involved in.

Vice-Commodore Colin Jacobs of the Royal Hamilton Yacht Club responded to a mailed query with information about the Greening family connection to the Yacht Club. Carla Pruden, nanny to both Bill and John Braden, sent some reminiscences in a letter to John Braden. The Registrar's Office at McGill University was good enough to fill in his academic career at McGill with a transcript.

The following people submitted to interviews either in person or over the telephone: Harcourt Bull (Will's cousin); Bob Hutcheson (who was present at Fairy Lake on the day that Will died); Ruby Moore (who worked at the H.S.R. with Bill); Dorelle Cameron (a friend of Gwyn Braden); Sis Wigle (the youngest sister of Bill's best friend, Bill Holton); Frank Cooke, who took over Bill's position at the H.S.R. upon his death, Betty Leggett who was the switchboard operator at the H.S.R.

Table of Contents

Chapter 1: Roots

The Braden family had its roots in Pennsylvania. A Jacob Braden served in the War of Independence, and was with Washington at Valley Forge and Brandywine, as well as at other engagements. On the maternal side, an ancestor was Colonel Robert Boyd, an Irish patriot, who was a persona non grata to the British governmental authorities, and was forced to flee to the United States to save his life. He brought with him his wife of a few months, Mary Robb Boyd, and they located in Philadelphia, where her brother was a jeweler.(1)

For the purpose of telling the story of the Canadian branch of the Braden family, it begins with James Braden, the seventh son of James and Elizabeth (Boyd) Braden, who was born in Greene County, Pennsylvania on 28 January 1825. He attended the common schools in the state until age sixteen. Young James had an additional three years of study at the academy located at Martinsburg, Ohio. He moved next to Kentucky, where he taught for a year in a private school near Frankfurt. He returned then to his native state, from where he received his matriculation at Jefferson College in Canonsburg, Pennsylvania. He was a graduate of the class of 1847 with a Bachelor of Arts degree. He next located at Georgetown, Kentucky, where for two years he was an instructor at Georgetown College, a Baptist institution. At the end of this period he moved back to Washington, Pennsylvania, where he began reading medicine under the tutelage of a Dr. Le Moyne, who would go on to establish in later years, the first crematory in the U.S.A. He joined the medical department of the University of Virginia at Charlottesville from where he graduated as a Doctor of Medicine in 1850. Doctor Braden would run his practice in Washington, Pennsylvania, from 1850-1863.(2)

His life dramatically changed in 1863 when he moved to the state of Indiana, where two of his brothers already resided. He established his home in Indianapolis, where he became one of the founders of the firm of William and James Braden, which was engaged in the book and stationery business. He retired from medicine to put himself wholeheartedly into running this business. In 1876, he moved to southern Indiana, and in 1883 he bought an interest in mineral springs at

West Baden. From 1883-1888, he was the Receiver of Public Moneys of the U.S. Land Office at Walla Walla, Washington. In 1888, he took his family back to Indiana, selling off his interest in the mineral springs and hotel property at West Baden, and resuming residence in Indianapolis. In his later years, Dr. Braden acquired extensive mining interests in the Rouge River valley of Oregon, and it was here while visiting his mines that Dr. Braden passed away.(3)

Dr. Braden was politically active in the Republican Party. When Garfield was the Republican presidential candidate, Dr. Braden was nominated to represent his district in Congress, but lost out. He was a member of the Presbyterian Church, and was affiliated with the Masons as well as the International Order of Odd Fellows (I.O.O.F.).(4)

His second marriage was to Miss Lydia Ellen Short on 4 September 1866. She had been an 1860 graduate of Northwestern Christian College, the second woman in the school's history to obtain a degree. They parented four children, three girls and a boy. Romaine was the first born (1867-1930), followed by Norman (b. 1869), and then Stella (1873-1958). A fourth child, Laura, passed away at age 10. They resided at 56 Downey Avenue in Irvington, Indiana, an Indianapolis suburb, in a house complete with a tower (turret), which in this era, was architecturally symbolic of having a degree of wealth.(5)

The parents believed in a liberal education for their children. Norman received his education at Whitman College in Walla Walla, Washington, followed by time at a business college in Indianapolis, until he became identified with electrical interests.(6)

When Dr. Braden died on 12 May 1907, he was the last survivor of a family of thirteen children. He was interred in Crown Hill Cemetery in Indianapolis.(7)

Norman Short Braden, his only son, is the next figure to follow as we trace the story of Bill Braden. He entered the employ of the Westinghouse Electric and Manufacturing Company at Cleveland in 1899, a career that would last until his retirement in April of 1944. Having left the Managership of the Cleveland office, he arrived in Hamilton in 1904 as the Sales Manager of the newly formed Canadian Westinghouse Company Limited. He would go on to hold roles in the Company that included Vice-President, and membership on the Board of Directors, ultimately reaching the position of Vice-Chairman of the Board in 1939. In addressing the Rotary Club of Hamilton at the Royal Connaught Hotel in 1934, Braden, in his role as Vice-President, spoke of the early days of the Company in Canada:

> The Canadian Company had been formed in 1897 to manufacture airbrakes
> …starting with 100 employees. Seven years later, the manufacture of electrical
> equipment was started, and the business increased till as many as 2500 employees

had been engaged when business was at its best....some of the larger pioneer achievements of his firm included the building of the five large hydro generators at Queenston, which at the time of their construction were the largest of their type in capacity in the world; the fitting up of the Steel Company of Canada with electrical equipment, making it the first steel mill in the world to be completely operated by electricity; the construction of all the electrical equipment for the Sarnia tunnel; the building of the hoisting equipment for International Nickel. Westinghouse engineers sent out the first radio broadcast of entertainment from station KDKA in November 1920, and had maintained this service to the present day. The Canadian company had initiated broadcast programs to the Arctic regions.(8)

He was eulogized by the Company President in the following manner:

....he was one of the pioneer members of our organization....His vision and foresight of what could be accomplished by the use of electricity in industry, railways and the home, helped in large measure the forward march of electrical power in this country....His genial presence will be missed at many...gatherings in the future. He...had taken an active interest in all Westinghouse employee activities.(9)

His grandson remembers that Mr. Braden was one of the moving forces in having car radios installed in automobiles; and one must ponder how socially this came to affect North American society!(10) This view is backed up by a letter that Mr. Braden wrote to the magazine Hardware in Canada in 1933:

....For automobile use, the radio sets, to give any degree of satisfaction, must be of good design, well made and not of the cheap construction which ordinarily applies to many small sets. We believe the best way to establish a fair selling price to the consumer is by maintaining the list of advertised prices for the entire radio season, which not only reassures the public , but gives the dealer a safe basis upon which to operate, and prevents complications in his time payment arrangements....(11)

When it came time to get married, Mr. Braden married into another well known Hamilton family that had roots in the business community as well. In 1799, Mr. Nathaniel Greening, at age twenty, left the Tintern Abbey Wire Mills, and moved to Warrington where he established a business in 'wire drawing'. His second son, Benjamin, served a seven year apprenticeship as a wire drawer, and then commenced business for himself, and continued till 1858, when he emigrated to Canada, and became one of the pioneers of the wire industry in this country, starting what became known as the B. Greening Wire Company Limited.(12) Benjamin Greening would have ten children, six of whom stayed in England, and four of whom took up residence in Canada. A grandson, Herald (b. 1880) would become 'the father of motorboat racing in Canada', and would play a key role in the life of young Bill Braden. The Greening name was one that was famous as part of the history of the Royal Hamilton Yacht Club. In 1888, his father, Samuel Owen Greening was part of a syndicate that owned the Yacht Club's first flagship. He was a charter member and Vice-Commodore when the Club became 'Royal' in 1891.(13) Young Greening himself got into the boating business back in 1904. He was returning home from a canoe trip up in Muskoka, when he decided to give up paddling and power his craft with an engine. Using a foot lathe in his attic, Greening built a 3 hp motor boat engine: the first one ever constructed in Canada. The engine would drive his canoe at the speed of 9 mph.(14) A columnist described him in the 1920s:

> ....There is perhaps no name better known in power boat racing circles than that of Harry B. Greening of Hamilton, Ontario....He has been an outstanding figure in the development of the high speed racing boat and in the upbuilding of this branch of the sport and the placing of racing on a higher plane of sportsmanship. Since the first **Rainbow** came out...he has built no less than four boats for the principal racing events in this county, the Gold Cup and the Fisher-Allison Trophy races. Keenly interested in the design of both boats and engines, he has striven in each of his boats for speed rather through the perfection of hull design than through the use of unlimited power. All of his boats have been fine looking craft, well designed and built, and extremely pleasing to look at, and all of them had speed....in September 1923, in **Rainbow III**, he established a record when he ran 1064 miles in 24 hours, the longest distance ever recorded for a vessel of any kind in that space of time.(15)

A writer looking at the 1923 boat racing season had these observations:

> One of the misfortunes of motor boat racing occurred during the Gold Cup race at Detroit. **Rainbow III**, owned and driven by Commodore H.B. Greening of the Royal Hamilton Yacht Club had won the first two 30 mile heats, and seemed to be on the way to win the third and final heat. She held the lead for the first twenty-five miles, and then lost a cotter pin out of the steering gear. She stopped for eight minutes to make repairs, but could not finish in better than fourth place. The total elapsed time for the ninety mile race was better for Packard Chris Craft (tied with **Rainbow**) and she was given the trophy. Everything else about **Rainbow III** functioned perfectly and it was only because of the faulty pin that she did not win the Gold Cup.

....It was back in 1923 that a record was established which has not been surpassed to this day. Commodore H.B. Greening...decided to set a real record. The plan was to set a record for twenty-four hours of continuous running. A fast boat like **Rainbow** could not be driven during darkness, so two twelve hour runs were determined upon running from 6 am to 6 pm on successive days. A course was laid out on Lake Rosseau, 9 ½ miles straightaway making the circuit equal to nineteen miles....(16)

Greening drove for 11 hours, 36 minutes and 5 seconds, at an average speed of 45.3 mph, to total the 1064 miles travelled.

Bill Braden Jr. recounted how there was a story that Gar Wood sent a gold cotter pin later on to Harry Greening, to commemorate that Gold Cup win.(17)

In 1925, Greening decided to make another attempt to surpass the 1923 record for a distance covered in 24 hours. Using his **Rainbow IV**, fitted with a Gar Wood marine engine, he approached the familiar course laid out again at Lake Rosseau. This time, he attained an average speed of 50.78 mph to establish a new distance record of 1218.88 miles.(18)

George Bernard, a Canadian scribe, had the following assessment of Greening's contribution to Canadian boating:

....There is a popular misconception that anyone with money can have the fastest boat in the world. Harry Greening is well off and has spent a tidy sum on motor boats, but his persistent, intelligent effort...has brought him to the fore where mere money would have held him forever in mediocrity.... unlike the vast majority of prominent Canadian and American racing men, Harry Greening does not benefit financially either directly or indirectly by any of his motor boat activities.

....Harry Greening began his hobby by building a two cylinder, two cycle marine engine when he was 21. In 1904, he travelled across Lake Muskoka at the 'hair raising speed' of 14 mph....His **Gadfly III** in 1912 attained the then phenomenal speed of 27 mph with 100 horsepower....Greening had a test tank in the basement of his house in which miniature models of proposed hulls were tested....(19)

Some of Harry Greening's feats include being named by the American Power Boat Association as one of the ten pioneers of motor boat racing in North America, and winning the Fisher Gold Cup in 1920 at Miami, with an accompanying prize of $5000. His **Rainbow II** bettered 60 mph in 1922, a top speed for its day. **Rainbow III** was conceded as the world's fastest boat in 1923. In

1929 with **Rainbow VII**, he drove 723.9 miles for a twelve hour record that stood for decades. In 1929, Greening won the Lipton Trophy donated for a North American championship race. (20) When Harry Greening passed away in Palm Beach, Florida, at age 80, in late February 1960, he was the Chairman of the Board of Directors of the B. Greening Wire Company Limited. He has begun working in the company in 1897. He worked in many Departments in the company, but his greatest interest was in the weaving section, and he himself was proud to have served an apprenticeship 'on the road' as a salesman. Shortly after the beginning of the 20th Century, he was appointed Superintendent, and on the death of his father in 1911, he became President of the company. At the time of his death, the Spectator noted "the Company maintained and increased its leading place in the industry. Today the firm can claim to process a broader range of alloys and wire sizes than any other mill in Canada and possibly North America.(21) Harry Greening would be inducted posthumously into the Canadian Motorsport Hall of Fame in 2003. He held the positions of Commodore of the Royal Hamilton Yacht Club and Chairman of the Racing Commission of the American Power Boat Association. He is also remembered for being the co-founder of International Airways, which became part of Canadian Pacific Airlines; and was a major player in the founding of the Hamilton Automobile Club.(22)

The last word on the effect that "Uncle Harry" had on the Braden family comes from Bill Braden himself:

….in company with my father and Harry Greening, I saw all of the Harmsworth races, starting from 1928 when Marion Carstairs brought over her **Estelle** fleet of boats right then to 1932 when Kaye Don made his second and last attempt to beat Gar Wood. When Harry Greening started getting interested in racing boats shortly after the first war, my father used to ride with him as his mechanic. I remember going for a ride in Harry Greening's **Rainbow IV** in the fall of 1924…. There is no doubt about it but that these spins in the early Rainbows gave me the bug.(23)

The Greening family, because of their lofty position in Hamilton society, were 'first' in many categories. They were the owners of a Robinson car, the first four cylinder car of American manufacture to be imported into Canada, prior to World War I. Its maximum speed was clocked at 30 m.p.h., in an era where the speed limit in the city was not much faster than the speed at which one could walk down the road.(24)

But returning to the story of the Bradens, it was Harold Greening's sister, Mabel (b. 1883), who would catch the fancy of Norman Braden, and they got married. From this marriage came three children. A daughter, Eleanore, was the first in 1911, followed by son William (b. 1915), who is the main character in this book, and then a second daughter, Margaret (b. 1916).

Chapter 2: Youth

Eleanore Braden was born on 30 December 1911. A little over three years later, Bill was born on 5 January 1915, weighing in at 6 lbs. 1 oz. In those years as the first children came along, Norman and Mabel Braden resided at 134 Duke Street in Hamilton.(1) A year after Bill's arrival, the family moved residence to 181 Jackson Street West.(2) At the time, Norman held the position of Sales Manager for Canadian Westinghouse Company Limited.

Norman Braden at his desk at Canadian Westinghouse @1930-1931.

Elementary School Years

In 1921, it was time for young Will to go off to school. The choice was Central School on Bay Street South in Hamilton, where he was in attendance until 1924. This was a school with which his family had had earlier ties: both his mother and Aunt Hattie Greening had both been students there. He changed schools in September 1924, moving to Brantdale School, on Mount Hamilton, where he stayed until 1926. Here Braden began his career of being strong in extracurricular activities, playing on the school baseball team, and singing in the school choir. He proudly noted in his diary that one Christmas, he played the role of Santa Claus.

Young Bill Braden @1918-1920.

Norman Braden stands on the front lawn of the family home, holding his daughter Margaret, while Bill stands to his father's left

In September 1926, he enrolled at Hillcrest School, a boys day school that had been set up to replace the famous Highfield, which had been established in 1901 at the foot of the Hamilton Mountain between Bay Street South and Ravenscliffe Avenue. Major John S. Hendrie, the Mayor of Hamilton, had been encouraged by the Governor-General, Lord Aberdeen and his wife, along with other leading Hamilton families to create a new private school for boys that would 'prepare able and privileged young men'. (3) The school had been in operation as both a day school and a boarding school, until a fire ravaged the site on 5 May 1918. The new school opened its doors in September 1920, in the eyes of many as a temporary structure, until Highfield could be recreated in a different location. It was located on the Russell property at the corner of Queen and Main Street in Hamilton. The school building used to belong to Cousin Ethel (Greening) Pantazzi's parents. Student population numbered sixty day students, half of what they had had in their previous building, with a complete loss of their boarding population.(4) Will remained there until he graduated with the class of 1929, in the last year of Hillcrest's existence, under the leadership of Headmaster Reverend "Eagle Beak" Heaven (as Will referred to him). Reading the names of his contemporaries in class photos, one recognizes people who would go on to be close to Bill Braden throughout the rest of his life: Basil Southam, Bill Holton, and J. Ridley Doolittle. A classmate from 1927-1928, who would go on to have a fascinating career in the Canadian aircraft industry was one Frederick Timothy Smye, who would become Vice-President of A.V. Roe (Canada) Limited, and be intimately involved in the Avro Arrow project in the late 1950s. Once again, involvement in school activities became the hallmark of Braden's time there. In 1927, he was a sub on the first football team. In 1928, he moved up to the position of 'inside' on the same team. In the winter of 1928-1929, he played with the school's first hockey team, anchoring one defensive position. He was very proud to don the school colors of 'green and white'. In the non sporting arena, in 1929, he represented his class in an oral composition, speaking in a church setting on the topic of 'the aeroplane'.

Other memories from that period include the family having a summer cottage on Hamilton Bay. There was another residential move when the family moved onto the Hamilton mountain in 1924, at 15 Westmount Avenue.(5) During his tenure there, Braden and his friend, Bill Holton, started their own business, called the 'White Star Pigeon Lofts'. The company letterhead described them as a 'Breeders of Fancy Pigeons' and a 'Member of the Canadian Pigeon Fanciers Association.' In 1929, he won the award for Best Collection in the Pigeon Show. 'Sis' Wigle, the youngest sister of Bill Holton, remembers that somewhere along the line, her brother and Will Braden did not do a good job of keeping the different breeds of pigeons separated from each other, and the business fell into disrepair.(6) As a child, at age eight, Braden had inherited 'asthma' from the Greening side of the family, and a consulting doctor had felt that he needed a project to entertain him for the number of hours he would be spending inside at home. Thus 'pigeons' came to be a part of his life at this young age.(7)

Young Bill also rode horses in his youth. The <u>Hamilton Spectator</u> had a photo of Bill in its 22 October 1925 edition under the banner of 'Rider of Promise', with a brief write up that noted: "The rider, who has shown outstanding talent in recent shows, is one of the star junior entries", and went on to show Bill on a jumping 'Sunrise'.(8) He was a contestant when the Wentworth County Hunt Club opened its winter season at the club arena in early January 1928. In the Class 2 Pony Jumping (horses of 12.2 hands in height or less) he was aboard 'Dolly Gray'. In the Handy Hunter Class (over a difficult course without wings to the jumps), he rode 'Sunrise'. He took the same horse to the 'Musical Chairs' competition. The <u>Mail and Empire</u> was lavish in its praise: ":….A big feature of the night was the handsome riding of some of the younger contestants, many of whom figured in the prize list. The ribbons were awarded following the events in the arena, and a social hour was greatly enjoyed."(9) Bill missed the Spring Horse Show in May, because the family was away on a European trip. In the 1929 Horse Show in Hamilton, he won the Seagram Trophy for Canadian Half Bred Hunters, and was recognized as 2nd Best Boy Rider.

Norman Braden on his horse 'Nauru' while young Bill sits astride 'Sunny' in the late 1920s.

Bill kept a hardback scrapbook in these years which was divided up between clippings and photos of horses, and of Harry Greening and race boats.

Secondary School Years

Will's secondary school years were spent at Trinity College School, the boys boarding school, in Woodstock, Ontario (1929-1930), and in Port Hope, Ontario (1930-1933). The school had been founded in 1865, and had a reputation as one of the most prestigious schools in the country. Braden attended during the time of the Headmastership of Dr. Orchard, and a number of Braden's contemporaries from his Hillcrest days joined him on campus, including Bill Holton who was his roommate for three of the four years on campus, and Dave Ambrose, who filled the same role in his last year there. Right from the outset, Bill found his niche playing sports at the school. In his first year, he was a member of the Littleside (under age 16) XIV football team, and received football colors (awarded for ability in that sport) for being a member of the school's fifth team, at the 'inside' position.. On the school's annual sports day, he came second in the 120 yard hurdles for Littleside (again under age 16).

He continued to show his abilities in the 1930 school year, again receiving his hockey colors for the fifth team, playing left defense. He showed academic prowess as well, receiving second general proficiency for the Lower Shell Form. At the Annual Sports Day in 1930, he showed an improvement by capturing the 120 yard hurdles for Middleside (the over age 16 students). At the Christmas exams in 1930, he placed ninth of seventeen in the Middle Remove (terminology from the old British Grammar School system). A section of the Grade 10 class was based on ability, in this case, the middle achievers (Bill was ninth in this group).(10) In 1931, he advanced to the second team in hockey (Middleside), and received his hockey colors for playing left defense, at the season's end.

In the 1931 Matriculation Results, Bill Braden was in the 'remove form', one level above the 'lower shell', the lowest grade in the senior school. He obtained passing grades in two of the six subjects he was taking. He played 'inside' on the Middleside third football team, and as well, was Captain of the Brent House football team. During the hockey season, Braden's name was a constant in 'The School' hockey lineup on defense, paired with Mr. Wynn on the blueline. At the end of the season, he once again received his hockey colors for his steady work on the Second Team. The spring of 1932 also saw him develop an expertise in musketry. It was noted that in the annual course of musketry: "Braden made the highest score of 97 out of 100". In two of the matches of the Dominion of Canada Rifle Association competition, Bill Braden came first in the Senior Division with a score of 96 in the first match.

In the Christmas Exam Order, Bill was in the lower 4th form (Grade 11), and stood ninth out of thirteen students in the class. At the Annual Sports Day in 1932, Bill Braden won the L. McMurray Cup for winning the 120 yard open hurdles in the Senior School (grades 10-13). He again received his football colors for his play with the Second Team, and he made the First team for whom he was a spare on the bench. He was also involved in House matches, playing 'inside' for his house (Brent House) in Bigside (the best of the over age 16 students). In the December 1932 exams, Braden passed three subjects which he could put towards his Ontario high school certificate. During the winter, Braden again played hockey, this time for the first team, where he was matched with Mr. Wynn as the main defense pairing for The School. The School <u>Record</u> hockey writer had this assessment of Braden's season: "W. Braden. Age 17. Left Defence. Worked very hard and frequently showed great possibilities. Was very weak at rushing and somewhat careless around the net. A fast skater and a fair body checker. He improved steadily throughout the season."(11) He again received his hockey colors for his first team efforts. Braden also became involved in a new sport in his senior year: boxing in the welter-weight division. He lost in his only competitive match. Again in this year, he won the J.L. McMurray Challenge Cup for 120 yard hurdles, open competition. Then at year end, the <u>Record</u> bid 'farewell' (Valete) To Will Braden, noting that he was in the 5th Form (Grade 12), and 2nd team football and 1st team hockey. He was also Captain of the Brent House baseball team, and had played cricket for Middleside. Outside of the athletic fields, Braden was also involved in extracurriculars. In 1932, he had a small part in the school play, as well as playing the piano in the school orchestra. In 1933, he moved on to play the saxophone in the orchestra. In the final Matriculation Results in June 1933, Bill as a member of the Middle School (Grade 12), was recommended by the school as having passed two courses. Remembering that in December 1932 he had attained three courses that would count towards the certificate, he totaled five of the necessary six courses.(12)

Bill Braden Jr provides an anecdote about his father's years at T.C.S.:

….He had a motorcycle while at school, and it could not be stored at the school. He could get off school property for two hours to go to the library: this was the camouflage he used to be able to go riding on his motorbike….My younger brother, John, used to go to the school in the mid 50s, and Dad used to visit the school to see how John was doing in sports. Dad would have been in the top half of the student body in sports in his era.(13)

To finish off his secondary school career, Bill's folks sent him to a special private school, Le Rosey, on the shores of Lake Geneva, at Rolle in Switzerland. To get there, Will left Quebec on 2 September 1933, aboard the Canadian Pacific passenger ship The Empress of Britain, arriving at Southampton five days later. While in England, there are a variety of pictures that exist, showing that Braden stayed with Stewart Chapman, at his home in Sussex, during his twelve days in the country. They shared some days out together: one at the West Sussex Golf Club, and a day at Brooklands watching a 500 mile road race. On the 19th of September, he flew out of London to Paris on a tri-motored Air France Golden Clipper airliner, which held the commercial speed record of 76 minutes for this route and the connecting flight force landed in a field near Lausanne, Switzerland. A Lausanne newspaper noted that there was a very low fog on the land, and that there were only four passengers on board. They continued the flight the following morning and arrived at Rolle later that day.(14) He was re-united with Stewart Chapman, who had been a colleague at Trinity College School. Various families whose children were contemporaries of Bill Braden, sent their children to this school at the same time (1933-1934). Another of his classmates was H.R.H. Crown Prince Mohamed Reza Pahlavi of Iran, who would later become famous or infamous as the Shah of Iran.

His marks were interesting, as were the subjects he was taking: he got an 8.5/10 for behavior, and a 7/10 for application (how well he tried or applied himself, with or without getting good grades), 7/10 in Chemistry, 7/10 in Physics, 5, 6.5, 4 in the three terms in Geometry, 7 in the last term of Trigonometry, 7 in Math specialty, 6.5 last term of Latin, 7,6,7 in the three terms for English, and 6 in the last term for French.(15) As he had done back in Canada, Will Braden made his mark in athletics. In 1933, he was left back on the school's first soccer team. In 1934, he played his favorite position of left defense on the first hockey team; and the team ended as runners-up in the Series 'B' League.

The Le Rosey hockey team, runners-up in the Intermediate Swiss Championship. Bill Braden is in the back row, second from the left. Photo taken on 14 February 1934.

As well, he made the school's first rowing team as a number two, ending third in the Open Competition at Geneva, and first in the competition at Montreux. He also turned out to be a good skier, obtaining a fourth place in the senior slalom on 6 March 1934, trailing the winner by a mere seven seconds, with a time of 1:28.(16) In the downhill, he fell. He was no slouch when it came to skating as well, winning the senior race. In the prognosis for the track and field season of 1934, the school newspaper had the following assessment of Bill Braden: "Among the senior runners, Bill Braden is our big hope; supple, elastic, he is capable of sustained effort without apparent fatigue. He runs like the wind, and his well-endowed 'mane' gives him the appearance of a young lion looking for space."(17) He also was noted to excel with the senior relay team, and in throwing the javelin.(18) From Braden's diary, it can be seen that these prognoses were not far off from the truth. He won the 100 meters race, the javelin throw, was the anchor man on the winning relay team, and captured the obstacle race. On the Pentecost holiday, 19-20 May 1934, there were a variety of sports occurring around the school.(19) Bill Braden was involved in the school's annual tennis tournament, both in singles and doubles competition. In the singles semi final, he came up against Pahlavi , and as the <u>Echo</u> stated: "Pahlavi, playing against Braden, pursued his winning way without serious trouble". In the doubles semi-final, it was noted that "Braden and Audibert had a great deal of worry and trouble before they eventually defeated the Clarks in a long drawn-out three set affair". Unfortunately, the final match had a similar ending as the singles match. The reporter stated:

> "In doubles, Metternich and Pahlavi gained the victory, which had been conceded to them on the basis of early form over Audibert and Braden. The match was very interesting to watch, for after the loss of the first set, the latter pair made a hard fight of it, and almost succeeded in taking the second. They evened the count at 5-all, before Metternich and Pahlavi could get the situation in hand and run out the set and the match. The final score was 6-2 and 7-5.(20)

Down at the water's edge, people were having trouble with the new skiff. As was reported: Metternich, having already tried it before, was able to keep his equilibrium better than his unlucky predecessors. He was however, pretty shaky and was quick to endorse Bill Braden's announcement that it wasn't as easy as it looks. To quote the gleaming-eyed Hamilton 'Tiger': "It looks like a snap when Johnnie's out there, but when you get in yourself, the darn thing wabbles so much that you hardly dare pull on the oars for fear you'll find yourself in the lake".(21) Braden lived in the L'Ermitage at Rolle; and the Reid Chalet at GStaad.

Bill Braden on the back steps of L'Ermitage at Le Rosey, Switzerland on 10 October 1933.

Bill Braden (rt) with an English school chum on 15 July 1934,
two days after purchasing his first Ariel motorcycle.

The year after finishing at Le Rosey, Bill Braden, now aged 20, decided to re-visit the school on a motorcycle with Rid Doolittle, a fellow T.C.S. grad from Hamilton. Doolittle wrote an unpublished manuscript about the trip, and gave credit to Braden for suggesting a motorcycle trip to Switzerland:

> One night last winter, fixing up our motorcycles in a cold garage, Will started one of his frequent rambles about Switzerland, waxing eloquent over the marvel of it all: "Gee Rid, wouldn't it be dandy if we could get across the pond, ride to Switzerland, and reach Le Rosey in time for the Old Boys Race on Sports Day…. if I could get a couple of breaths of that fresh, sootless Swiss air, I could lick anyone". Immediately, we started to work, first on figures, then on our fathers, and 'wow' what joy then, at last , facts, figures and fathers all agreed. It took a lot of skilful reasoning to convince the last, but not the least of the three, that we were capable of looking after ourselves in foreign countries….on June the 12th [1935], our parents waved a fond farewell. (22)

Bill Braden on his Ariel motorcycle that he rode across Europe in the summer of 1935.

The trip was not an uneventful one. As they pulled out of harbor, their passenger ship was hit by the collier Kafiristan, and they were both haunted by the thought of being involved in another "Titanic" style disaster at sea. In the end, three sailors off of the collier lost their lives, and the liner progressed safely on its journey....

After a brief stay in England, they got off of the cross-Channel ferry and traversed the French countryside, where in many communities the populace were unsure as to whether or not they were Americans. The duo motored on through Italy. They had no problems in this dictator-led nation until they arrived in the Eternal City:

> ....my attention was attracted by Will, being apparently escorted across the street by a man in plain clothes, so I called out: 'who's your friend?' 'Oh I don't know, some little wart that has been bothering me while I tried to look at the monument, but who's that damn fool standing up there beside you?' Immediately the two of us realized that we were under arrest by two plain clothes men, but for what? Well that was beyond us both....It was not until [later] we were told that due to the present British-Italio feeling....it was probably because they saw the English license plates [on the two motorcycles] that we were arrested as spies, being at the time of arrest, just across the road from Benito Mussolini's office....(23)

The boys had a measure of revenge on leaving for Switzerland:

....Four hours later, we were leaving the Italians, with heavy consciences and fear in our hearts as we had succeeded in taking pictures of their field guns, camouflaged in strategic positions on the old St. Bernard Pass. By the fifth hour, we had reached the peak of Mount St. Bernard, and were starting down into Switzerland. (24)

Then it was a race to get there on time for the Old Boys Race on Sports Day, and the motor bikes did not let them down:

Will, pepped up with the Swiss air, as the race horse is doped from the blue bottle, ripped off his windbreaker and shoes, and stepped out to the starting line, dressed in filthy grey flannels, bug smeared shirt, and stocking feet, just as the starter was squeezing the trigger....Will, sorting himself out from the rest of the crowd, broke into the lead and set a beautiful pace, until his swelled chest broke the ribbon at the finish....As I ran up to embrace and congratulate my partner, fashion and society looked on with a questioning smile at these rogues of the road, gone mad with victory. At 8000 feet in the Alps, here in the middle of summer, we might have gone skiing had we been prepared....(25)

Doolittle added other memories of their time in Switzerland:

We stayed two days at the school and had frequent swims in the waters of Geneva....On Sunday July 1st, accompanied by three students from the school, we went to Berne to see the famous Swiss Grand Prix- a motorcycle road race. The bikes hit speeds of 100-110 m.p.h....At 8000 feet, we visited the Rhone Glacier, and dodged crevices that were fifty to sixty feet deep.(26)

The next stop was Germany, and the lads were quite sensitive to where they were, after the unexpected experience of being in Mussolini's Rome: "...we crossed the red line and found ourselves in enemy territory, strictly verboten by our parents. We didn't know whether to be scared as we tore through the so-called DMZ, or treat it as just any other country".(27)

In looking back on the trip, Bill Braden's comments shed light on how he would lead his future life:

....All kidding aside, Rid, that was the most marvelous trip I ever hope to make. Organized tours, trains, buses from now on are all taboo, and all I ever want is just a cycle (with a good motor)...which I can own and operate myself, go where I like, when I like....(28)

Post-Secondary Education

Bill moved on to attempt to obtain his university degree. He first attended McMaster University for two years (1934-1936). In the first year, he entered the Arts Program, and played hockey on the school team. The hi-light of the season was a hockey trip to Ann Arbor, Michigan. Academically, he received credits in Geometry, Trigonometry, Latin, and Chemistry. In his sophomore year , he tried out for the senior football team, and he obtained credits in Geology, French, a second Geology, Bible, History and English. He then moved onto McGill for the 1936-1937 school year, where he got credits in two different economics courses. However, he did not obtain credits in English, Philosophy and Psychology, which left him short on credits to obtain his B.A. In 1936, he became a member of the McGill Chapter of the Alpha Delta Phi Fraternity.

Braden was an individual who was desirous of remembering people he met on his travels. In his personal papers, he kept a green hardcover scrapbook, in which he inscribed people's names, and how he had met them. His anecdotal reflections are fascinating to read: a White Russian is remembered as "a very interesting chap, was with a gang of seven or eight American girls". Another man "won a ping pong tournament" on board ship; while another "[I] was with him on a shuffleboard tournament". He had an eye for the women as well: a girl named Tessie was described as "quite large"; while another one had a "hot bod", and a third was "blond and a peach".(29)

When he returned from his trip overseas, Will was interested in fulfilling the dream of doing more travels on his motorbike. Along with his buddy Fred Southam, he toured both the western U.S.A., and western Canada from 30 May to 6 July 1936. Photos in his album register stops in Arizona at the Grand Canyon, San Francisco, Yellowstone Park (with eight photos showing the required close ups of a bear or bears), Vancouver, and Banff.

In 1937, there was a family trip to Atlantic City, highlighted by some evocative pictures of Bill on the boardwalk with his mother. At Easter 1938, there was a family skiing trip to Mount Washington in New Hampshire.

Bill Braden sitting with his Mom on the boardwalk at Atlantic City, New Jersey on 12 May 1937. Atlantic City was a popular spot to visit for two generations of the Braden family.

How did Joan McColl and Bill Braden come to meet? It seems that Joan and her childhood friend, Dorelle Cameron, had been both keen figure skaters, and members of the Toronto Skating Club in the 1930s. Also members of the club, were an attractive pair of sisters, the Taylor girls, whose blond curls and extravagant costumes attracted much attention during the skating parties. One day, Joan proudly reported to Dorelle that she had a new beau, having snagged him away from Barbara Taylor. Dorelle stated that "she seemed very pleased with herself"(30) There would be an interesting story as to how Bill Braden came to meet this young lady in Toronto, when he was living with his parents on the Hamilton Mountain, but there does not appear to be anyone left alive who could fill in those details….

Joan McColl's father died of tuberculosis when she was age 12. Her grandfather had an oil refinery in Toronto, called 'McColl Brothers'. It was later called 'McColl-Frontenac' (31), and was bought up by Texaco. Mrs. McColl would come to remarry a gentleman named Francis Farwell, who would come to play a key role in the Bill Braden story.

In a scrapbook kept by Bill Braden, there is a newspaper engagement announcement, with pictures of the young couple. Under the title of 'Interesting Engagement', it was revealed that "the wedding of Miss Joan Gwendolyn McColl, daughter of Mrs. Francis Farwell, Toronto, and Mr. William Greening Braden, son of Mr., and Mrs. Norman S. Braden, Hamilton, is taking place on December 2 [1939] in Grace-Church-on-the-Hill, Toronto.(32) The engagement was officially announced on 12 March 1939.

Though there is no correspondence between the young couple that has survived, some of the ever-present Braden photos provide visual descriptions of their engagement period. There are photos from November 1938, with the caption: "4 months before engagement with 36 Ford Omelette in background".(33) Other photos from September 1939 show Joan and a girlfriend in swimsuits on the quay at a lake.(34)

When the wedding was held, socially it merited coverage in both the <u>Globe and Mail</u> as well as the <u>Hamilton Spectator</u> on the subsequent Monday. The <u>Globe</u>'s coverage was under the banner of "Miss Joan G. McColl Married to William Greening Braden At Choral Wedding Ceremony", and included a photo of the couple at the church with a banner "Pretty Bride of December First". (35) The write-up in the <u>Spectator</u> opens with the interesting phrase: "A wedding of wide interest took place Saturday afternoon….(36) The newspaper's description speaks of an era where every detail of a wedding was breathlessly anticipated by the readership:

> The service was fully choral, and the Rev. John H. Dixon conducted the ceremony. Mr. H.G. Langlois was at the organ. The choir boys preceded the bridal party down the aisle singing 'Praise My Soul The King of Heaven'. During the signing of the register, they sang 'O Perfect Love'.

> The bride, given in marriage by Mr. Francis Farwell, was lovely in a Molyneaux gown of duchess satin, with softly molded waistline and hips and fell into a graceful skirt and very long train. The sleeves long and close fitting to points over the hands were finished with seed pearl embroidery, which also outlined the square neckline. Her veil of Alencon lace was held to her head with orange blossoms and seed pearls, and she carried a bouquet of white orchids and lilies of the valley.(37)

Bill Braden and Joan McColl on their wedding day 2 December 1939.

Interestingly enough, the groomsmen included many familiar names from Will Braden's life: Bill Holton (of pigeon fame) was the best man, and the ushers included Lieutenant John McColl (the bride's brother, who would go on to be a Canadian Spitfire pilot during World War II), Flight Lieutenant Douglas Wigle, Fred Southam, David Ambrose, Ridley Doolittle, and cousin Owen Greening. In the family archives can be found a 16mm color film of the wedding reception. It would be interesting to speculate on the cost of having 16 mm color film shot for a 1939 wedding in an era where color photography was in its infancy. One of the fascinating traditions in a wedding in this era, was where all the bride's gifts were laid out on long tables at the reception so it could be seen what gifts she received, and who gave what gift as well....The couple honeymooned in Havana, Cuba.

After the couple returned from their honeymoon, they settled down at 145 Kent Street in Hamilton, while their new house was being built on a property, along the escarpment in

Waterdown, given to them by his new stepfather-in-law, Francis Farwell.(38) In looking at where the family had its home, and its size, John Braden remarked: "My parents must have planned on having a large family. So they filled it up."(39) And so they did, the first child, young Billy, arriving on 23 September 1940. The second son, John, came on 9 March 1942, at 8:05 a.m. at Toronto General Hospital, while Will was overseas with the Canadian Army.

Up until Bill Braden volunteered to go overseas with the Canadian Army, he had been steadily employed by the B. Greening Wire Company in Hamilton, or as Bill described it in his Application for Commission Questionnaire: "At present employed at B. Greening Wire Co. Ltd. Hamilton, in sales office with view to learning the business and eventually handling the sales end. Worked in factory of the firm prior to going into the office. (Started in this firm after leaving McGill).(40)

Chapter 3: The War Years

Just as with many other young Canadians, Bill Braden decided to volunteer himself and his skills to the nation to help defeat the Nazis in World War II. At age 26, he was somewhat older than most volunteers of the period.

The first mention of Bill Braden's name in National Defence records is an application for a commission sent to the Officer Administering the Royal Canadian Ordnance Corps in Ottawa, and forwarded at the request of Mr. Francis Farwell.(1) The application contains some interesting facts. Braden had no previous military training, save for four years in the Cadet Corps at Trinity College, where he had attained the rank of Cadet Sergeant. The Interviewing Officer, Lieutenant-Colonel R. Neate, Officer Commanding No. 2 Detachment, R.C.O.C. made the following remarks about the applicant: "Well set-up young man. Smart in appearance, and appeared above the average in intelligence. Is not a mechanical Engineer but has been very interested in engines as a hobby (mostly gasoline engines)...."(2)

Less than a week later, his name came up again in military correspondence:

> ...provided he is found to be medically fit, for a recommendation for his appointment as Lieutenant (Assistant Ordnance Mechanical Engineer) to be forwarded to National Defence Headquarters through the District Officer Commanding, Military District No. 2. The services of this gentleman are required in the branch of the Master-General of the Ordnance (Chief Ordnance Mechanical Engineer office) National Defence Headquarters, at the earliest possible date.(3)

The following week, Braden was recommended for appointment to the Corps Reserve of Officers in the Royal Canadian Ordnance Corps, with the rank of Temporary Lieutenant (Ordnance Mechanical Engineer). He received a medical and was found fit for 'Category A'. The details of the physical exam help bring the man to life for the reader. He was 5' 10 ½" tall, weighing 150 lbs., with hazel eyes, brown hair, and fair complexion. His vision was 20/20 in both eyes, and his hearing was the same in both ears. His chest size was 39 inches, and his development was 'good'. He had two small scars on his right wrist, and in the past had suffered from bronchitis/asthma, kidney/bladder disease, and had worn glasses. Reflexes were normal, and he was not color-blind.(4)

Once he passed his medical, the process sped up:

> ...I am to inform you that it is desired that the name of W.G. Braden, 145 Kent St., Hamilton Ont., be added to the list of candidates for appointment to the Corps Reserve of Officers, R.C.O.C. (R.F.) M.D. 2 and attachment to No. 9 Detachment R.C.O.C., Ottawa, for training, with a view to appointment as Lieut. (Asst. O.M.E.) R.C.O.C. (A.F.) in the Ordnance M.T. Inspection section. The matter of the appointment of Mr. Braden has been the subject of correspondence between the Officer Administering R.C.O.C., and the Officer Commanding No. 2 Detachment R.C.O.C. direct.(5)

Temporary Lieutenants Braden and Basil Southam were to proceed to Ottawa by motor car and to report to Major Johnstone at the New Post Office Building in Ottawa, on 20 February 1941.(6) At the outset, he was drawing subsistence allowance of $1.70 per day, which was followed by the drawing of an additional 50 cents per day.(7) Will Braden then went off on a variety of war related courses, starting with a lecture on 'Common to All Arms Motor Transport' put on for one week (21-28 February 1941) by Number 9 Detachment R.C.O.C. A few days later, a three and a half week course was offered by the C.A.C.T.C. at Camp Borden, entitled 'Lectures on Common to All Arms, Motor Transport, Motorcycles and Tanks'. As soon as that course was completed, Ford Motor Company held a three and a half week course on 'Canadian Military Ford Vehicles'. This was immediately followed by a three day tour through the Chrysler plant. When that was done, General Motors offered a three and a half week course on 'Canadian Military Chevrolet Vehicles'.

While Braden was augmenting his knowledge of military transport, there was a variety of correspondence that transpired as to exactly when he should be taken on strength, and paid by the Army. The letters laid out the timeline of his signing up, noting that his Medical Board was on 17-1-41; that he received orders from Military District No. 2 to get his uniform and report back on 7-2-41; he then discontinued his civil employment on 17-2-41; and reported back to Military District No. 2 on 18-2-41; before he reported to Ottawa on 20-2-41, as noted previously. The letter goes on to state:

> ....As this Officer was promised, when interviewed, that he would not suffer financially during the period between leaving civil employment and receiving

his commission, it is felt that every consideration should be employed in having this Officer taken on the strength as of 18-2-41, please. As this gentleman is a specialist, it was necessary to give the assurance…in order that his services might be secured.(8)

Bill and Joan Braden in April 1941, before his departure overseas.

Braden was to be the Assistant Ordnance Mechanical Engineer and Lieutenant in the Corps Reserve of Officers in the Royal Canadian Ordnance Corps. in Military District No. 2, effective 1 February 1941; and was to be attached to No. 9 Detachment of the R.C.O.C.'s Mechanical Transport Section as of 18 February 1941. Subsequently, orders changed, and he was posted to No. 7 Detachment R.C.O.C. in connection with Mechanical Transport maintenance at St. John, New Brunswick. He travelled east as of 15 May 1941, once again in the company of his good friend, Basil Southam, who was also posted to the same unit, in the latter's motor car.(9) Their appointment was effective 16 May 1941. A newspaper report out of St. John, New Brunswick on 12 August 1941 in Bill Braden's personal photo album noted that he had been designated the new officer in charge of the ordnance workshop in the Golden Ball garage in town, and that he would also be acting as the accounting officer there.(10)

Once again, this shift from the Reserve Force to the Active Force flummoxed the Army paper pushers, who were responsible for paying his salary:

> Information is requested, please, as to whether the appointments of these officers to the Active Force have ever been promulgated in Gazette or Supplement to Routine Orders. The District Paymaster advises that to date these officers have not received clothing allowances, and that Ledger Sheets received indicate that they have only been in receipt of advances of pay.(11)

The District Paymaster needed the number of the Gazette in which Braden had been promulgated as a member of the Active Force so that he could pay out a clothing allowance to the Lieutenant. Three months later, there was still controversy as to paying his salary, and the exact dates from which it was to be paid:

> The District Paymaster, M.D. No. 7 advises that they were taken on strength of No. 9 Detachment R.C.O.C., effective 21-2-41. As there was apparently no authority for their salary, they were paid in the form of advances. Routine Order mentioned above, authorizes payment of their salaries from the 15th and 16th of May, 1941, but does not take into account any previous period. May this matter be adjusted please.(12)

The Army wanted to establish a Mechanical Transport Inspectorate, and had the names of some officers in mind to fill the roles. However, they were unavailable. Lieutenant Braden's name was put forth for consideration.(13)

He was next sent on a four month course (17 May to 8 September 1941) at the Motor Transport Workshop of #2 Detachment R.C.O.C. This was at Military District #1's Mechanics Training Centre in London and was a Course on General Motors Aircraft and Diesel Engines. After the completion of this course, he was sent on two weeks embarkation leave; and then was designated to attend the special Universal Carrier Course at the Ford Motor Company's Windsor plant, starting on 3 October 1941, and carrying on for five days. Colonel Thompson went on to write: "It is desired that these officers be placed on draft for the next available sailing after the completion of their Carrier Course". (14) On the very next day after this course was finished, the R.C.O.C.T.C. started a three week course on Harley-Davidson motorcycles. Once again, the paperwork followed them around the country:

....I am to inform you, the marginally named officers, at present attending the Carrier course at the Ford Motor Company's plant in Windsor, Ontario, have been elected to proceed overseas to fill vacancies on establishments. It is requested that these officers be instructed to proceed, on completion of their course October 3rd, to Military District No. 2 where they will be attached temporarily to No. 2 Det. R.C.O.C. or No. 2 District Depot, pending their departure overseas....On arrival in England, they will report to Canadian Military Headquarters, London.(15)

With his overseas departure set back, Braden was instructed next to proceed to the R.C.O.C. Training Camp, at Barriefield, where arrangements were made for him to receive an intensified motorcycle course. He was posted from No. 7 Detachment R.C.O.C. to No. 2 District Depot R.C.O.C. as of 25 October 1941. The question came up about possible embarkation leave: "...it was understood these officers would take their leave at the completion of their course at the motor companies. If this was not done, there seems to be no objection to their going on leave on completion of their course at the R.C.O.C. Training Centre provided time is available."(16) Again after this shift of Military Districts, his file is full of a series of letters regarding his pay and who was responsible to pay him. Interestingly enough, he was receiving a dependents allowance of $57 per month.(17)

Bill Braden Jr shared with me a story he had heard about his father's embarkation overseas on 31 October 1941, and it was not told to him by his mother. The train left Toronto for Halifax, with the wives accompanying their husbands as they headed east. The train either stopped just outside of Halifax, or somewhere along the rail line within the city limits. Wives were told that there would be a farewell reception at a city hotel, and that the husbands would be kept on the train in order to receive further information or were being delayed. The wives departed for the designated hotel in Halifax, and the train moved on to a different junction, where the husbands were re-routed to the ship. While the wives cooled their heels at the hotel, the boat pulled away from its berth. After a time the women came to question the delay, and were told to go to the docks for more information. They could see the ship disappearing in the distance. It was a devious act, and not a pleasant departure, for it was impossible for the ladies to say 'goodbye' to their men.(18)

In mid-November, orders came from the Assistant Quartermaster-General at Canadian Military Headquarters, designating Bill Braden as a R.C.O.C. Reinforcement Officer to be attached to 1 Division Ordnance Workshop for training.(19)

At the end of February 1942, a memo asked that Braden be posted to the Mechanical Transport Inspectorate at the Canadian Military Headquarters, which was being established: "C.M.H.Q. Administrative Order No. 26, dated 28 January 1942...authorizes Captain Mattson to command this unit, while Lieut. Highfield and Lieut. Braden are to cover off vacancies...."(20)

Captain Mattson soon saw the quality of officer he was getting with Lieutenant Braden, and three months later, he made a recommendation for promotion: "Please find my recommendation for the promotion of two of my subalterns to become Captains. These two Lieuts. are probably my best and most promising officers, and in my opinion are far superior to any of our R.C.A.S.C. Officers in our Inspectorate."(21) Canadian Military Headquarters had this view of Braden's promotion to Captain:

> Although Lieut. Braden is 7th on the seniority list of A.O.M.E.s, he was selected for posting to the M.T. Inspectorate because of his particular training with A & B Vehicles…which particularly qualified him for duties required of an officer on this unit. It is accordingly recommended that this promotion be given effect as of 8 March 42, that date at which this officer was T.O.S. M.T. Inspectorate.(22)

Bill was busy shooting pictures of places and fellow soldiers while in England, as well as gathering souvenirs of the places he visited. In January 1942, he was in Horsham, Sussex; while another album contains a ticket for a Ball sponsored by the Crawley and Horsham Hunt on 20 February 1942, with dancing to begin at 8:30 p.m. He wrote on the bottom of the ticket: "Joan hunted once with this hunt".(23) Bill possessed an advertising brochure from the East Hill Hotel, in Liss, Hampshire. On it, Bill had written: 'peacetime', and after almost seven decades, one cannot be sure that the Braden family had not stayed there during their 1938 trip to England. The brochure was written by the proprietor, John Morley, and stated:

> This is an invitation to you to come and stay for as long as you like in my hotel in Hampshire. East Hill is half-a-mile from Liss Station on the main London to Portsmouth line from Waterloo.…You won't find a marble swimming bath ….nor yet a lounge full of old 'tabbies'. But you *will* find enormous bedrooms, good beds (which cost me a fortune), bathrooms galore…a warm house and rather good food.…I can give you horses to ride and you can play golf all day at Liphook. The H.H. hunt all round East Hill.…When you come, let me know beforehand, so that I can light a fire in your room, and be there to open the front door.(24)

There was a subsequent letter from March 1942. Will wrote on it 'wartime', and 'arrived 25 March 1942'. Mr. Morley noted:

> Present conditions being as they are, we are doing our best to 'stay put' and to offer a home to those who perhaps for Services reasons, perhaps because their own homes are in uncomfortably hot areas, wish for the time being a temporary home. We cannot maintain our pre-war standard of luxury and rich food, but we do all we can in these difficult times. To compensate as far as possible for the reduced standard we have…actually reduced our prices.…(25)

One can understand the attractiveness of such a hotel to a man who has experienced the 'better things in life', and who has been living at Canadian Military Headquarters, in close proximity to a variety of other Canadian soldiers. It would be a great place at which to spend part of one's leave....

In April 1942, Lieutenant-General Andy McNaughton, Commander of the First Canadian Army laid the cornerstone of the Canadian Base Ordnance Depot, which was built to handle all big maintenance and repair jobs for the Canadian Army. As the newspaper wrote about it:

....The depot, pride of the Royal Canadian Ordnance Corps, is an enormous place, looking like a series of huge factory buildings and is being erected by the Royal Canadian Engineers. It is one of the sappers' major jobs in England; and probably will be completed by June [1942]. They started it at the end of 1941.

Between thirty and forty senior officers and several hundred soldiers watched the ceremony as the General laid the stone at the corner of one of the buildings. Overhead were signs 'Halifax Street' and 'Toronto Avenue', indicating the names of two streets that joined there.

'It is a very happy occasion to have the privilege of laying this cornerstone' said the Army Commander. 'It represents a magnificent accomplishment by the Royal Canadian Engineers by giving us in so short a time a facility which the army here has needed so much.'

He praised the work of the Ordnance Corps and said at this depot it would have the finest mechanical equipment to carry out its job.(26)

Braden soon received a promotion after being overseas some six months. According to Canadian Army Overseas R.O. 2105, dated 5 June 1942; and Overseas R.O. 2193, dated 26 June 1942, Braden was promoted to the rank of Captain, with the date of effect to be 8 March 1942. This was written up in the Hamilton Spectator, with an accompanying photograph.(27) In mid-November 1942, Braden was reclassified from A.O.M.E. Mechanical Transport to Captain (Mechanical) Officer according to Overseas R.O. 2742 of 13 November 1942.

In June 1942, Will Braden and a colleague visited H.M.S. Victory in Portsmouth harbor. Braden brought home five postcards from his visit, including both views of the place where Nelson fell on deck, and where he expired below deck. He also had postcards from where the Mechanical Transport unit operated at Bordon. One geographic locale was called 'The Devils' Punch Bowl', and underneath the postcard, Braden inscribed in ink: "On Guildford-Portsmouth Road. CTS used for Motorcycle Cross Country Training. Bad Fogs!'(28) Another postcard showed the

Royal Artillery Married Quarters at Bordon, with Braden inscribing: 'C.T.S. use this for men's quarters'(29) There are three postcards from Eastbourne. One of the cards shows the prewar beach and pier. Will has written in ink where the pier was cut back in order to prevent German invasion vessels from being able to tie up, where tank traps were dug in the sand, and where barbed wire was stretched to pen in the invader on the beach.(30) There were six postcards from the small village of Beeding. His inscription is dated August 1942, and notes; "Many units stationed around here".(31) Since this was the month of the failed landing by the Canadian Army at Dieppe, there is little wonder that there were many Canadian units in the area!

On September 1st, 1942, he was involved in motorcycle racing at Epsom. On the following day, he was inspecting landing craft at Shoreham. Like all Canadians in Great Britain, one tried to go on leave in London. Will got there in October 1942, and attended two plays. One was "DuBarry was a Lady" starring Frances Day and Arthur Riscoe. This comedy with music and lyrics by Cole Porter was being staged at His Majesty's Theatre in Haymarket, S.W. 1. The other play was "The Belle of New York", set in the New York City of 1898, and was put on at the Coliseum in Charing Cross. Also on 18 October 1942, Will participated in a twenty mile (ten lap) 500 c.c. motorcycle scramble (novice division) at Bagshot Heath, sponsored by the Streathern Motorcycle Club. In order to enter, he borrowed his friend Ted Frost's 1937 model 350 c.c. H.V. Comp Norton. In addition, he wore a Canadian Lieutenant's helmet and a woman's goggles. He noted in his album that wearing number 66, he fell on the fourth lap, and after re-starting, he finished 12th (last) out of 24 entrants. The only other Canadian entrant crashed into a tree on the first lap and was out of the race at that point.(32)

There was a write-up in his scrapbook about a German bomb wrecking a restaurant in a Home Counties town; while at the same time, a German twin-engine aircraft shot up their headquarters, at Bordon, Hants., while he was in it.(33) The raid was described years later:

> ....Twenty miles to the east, A single Dornier [217 E-4---a twin engine bomber] came in low and fast over Reading to scatter its bombs without warning in the center of the town. In Friar Street, the People's Pantry in the arcade was packed with diners when a direct hit completely demolished the building, blowing away the southern end of the Town Hall opposite. It was Reading's greatest hour of trial and when the final count was made, 41 persons had lost their lives....(34)

Even while Will was overseas and in the midst of a world war, he never lost his interest in automobiles and motor bikes. He received a letter from Mr. R.A. Jensen, the Managing Director of Jensen Motors, in West Bromwich, responding to Braden's request for reading literature on their 3 ½ litre Jensen auto. Since it was wartime, there were not many copies abounding: "...we are only able to forward you a limited amount of literature....", but these enclosures included typed specification sheets and data, as well as copies of road tests from 1936 and 1938. Two months later in another post, they forwarded Braden the names of two people living in Los Angeles, who owned such a car.(35) Similarly there was correspondence with Mr. Anthony Brooke of London, England, who was interested in selling his 4.9 litre Bugatti, who wrote to Will: "I'm very interested in your project to take the car to Canada: a damn good move to start up some enthusiasm for motoring in its proper sense. Some very successful Bugatti special engine motors have been run in Australia for years now."(36)

A formal portrait of Captain W.G. Braden, done in London, England in 1943

On leave on 14 March 1943, he was at Petersfield. Photos place him at Canterbury Cathedral on the 3rd of April. Will was in attendance at the 'Wings for Victory' Show and Gymkhana, held on Saturday 17 April 1943 at the Lees Farm, near Odiham. In pen, he marked on the brochure "Art Kilgour and I got one horse n. Gr. 1." On Thursday 3 June 1943, Will attended 'Derby Day' at the Epsom Races, as part of the May 29th to June 5th 'Wings For Victory Week', with profits from the week's events going to support the R.A.F. Benevolent Fund. Four races were run on this evening, with three of them being one quarter mile in length and the fourth race one of three furlongs. One group of photos shows his leave period from 27 June to 4 July 1943, which included time spent at the East Hill Hotel as well as at the Imperial Hotel in Torquay, Devon, England, from 30 June to 2 July, where the family had stayed at the time of the July 1938 Duke of York race. Time was also spent on 2 July in Dartmouth, where the Royal Navy College could be found; and on Hayling Island. During his stay at these towns, Braden would purchase post cards, whose photos augmented the ones he was taking. He also attended four races in August; and had a visit to the Thames River, where time was spent with Ted Frost and his wife, Doris, and their sailboat. In September 1943, it was back to the East Hill Hotel to attend the Prince of Wales garden fete. Also that month, he and a colleague went through Winchester Cathedral, and six postcards were picked up to commemorate the visit. In October, he attended the Ascot horse race. Also in that month, they were involved in a military exercise called 'Pirate'. On 5 December 1943, he entered a motorcycle trial competition. Driving a W.D. Norton and wearing #86, out of 99 entries, Braden finished 13th. During a December weekend, Bill and Art Kilgour stayed at the Blue Lantern Club in Forest Row, Sussex. Bill wrote in his album: 'good food, drinks'. They had several guests while they were on site, including the Chapman family. Later on in the month, there was a R.E.M.E. (R.C.O.C.) field day and demonstration held at the Redhill Memorial Sports Ground on 15 December. After an initial march past, teams of twelve men were involved in a contest to erect in the quickest time, a portable workshop shelter. At the same time on other areas of the ground, there was a tug of war; a blacksmithing contest where teams of two blacksmiths and one helper had to erect a blacksmith shelter and forge, and then hand forge a piece of work based on a sketch. As well, there was a vehicle fitting contest where teams of three men changed the front axle assembly of a 30 cwt lorry. Finally, there was a workshop demonstration, which showed off work in machinery. Thirty minutes after those five stations were set up, there was a driving contest where each team of two soldiers would back a 30 cwt lorry over a marked out course without the benefit of a rear view mirror to guide them. One hour later, the final pull in the tug of war was set to go off. The final activity was the officers' novelty race, where the officers commanding the workshops were to compete in a half mile bicycle race. This event would have provided a lot of interest for the Other Ranks, who were both interested in ensuring that their workshop was supreme, and who were more than willing to heap abuse on officers who did not ride the way the soldiers felt the bikes should be ridden. The day was finished by 11 am, with the presentation of awards, and the playing of God Save The King. Will captured key moments of the day on film. Similar photos to the ones he took, but taken from a different angle were placed in Canada Weekly for 14 January 1944.(37)

In October 1943, C.M.H.Q. desired to post Major H.B. Mattson from his command of the M.T. Inspectorate to command of No. 2 Canadian Recovery Company, R.E.M.E. Captain Braden was 2 i/c of the M.T. Inspectorate. Major Mattson wrote of his second in command: "This officer has acted as 2 i/c since 12 Oct 42 and has shown himself capable of commanding this unit. He is reliable, responsible, and of excellent character."(38) He further signed on the second page to the accompanying paragraph:

> I hereby certify that this officer can satisfactorily ride a motorcycle, drive any vehicle with which his unit is equipped, carry out maintenance tasks prescribed for drivers of his unit, and has demonstrated by the condition of the vehicles of the unit under his command that he possesses a sound knowledge of the care, maintenance and control of mechanical transport and a due sense of responsibility therefore.(39)

Braden's final promotion was chronicled in the 16 December 1943 Hamilton Spectator, which noted that he had been raised to the rank of Acting Major (Mechanic Officer), with effect from 10 November 1943. This was later upgraded to Major (Mechanic Officer) as of 1 March 1944 in Overseas Routine Order 4371. The confidential memo that accompanied this promotion noted: "The services of this officer have been satisfactory and it is now recommended that he be confirmed in the rank of Major (Mech Offr) effective 1 March 1944.(40)

Photos from 2 January 1944 illustrate the East Hill Hotel, and chronicle a visit from Owen Greening. In February, during the week after Valentine's Day, Will attended the Sadler's Wells Ballet. During that week, he might have seen the famous ballerina, Margot Fonteyn, who was one of the artists performing. In March, there are more photos from the East Hill Hotel including one of Basil Southam on a motorcycle with another Canadian bike rider. In March 1944, there was a series of photographs of the Motor Transport Office and Headquarters at Elder School House, in Bordon, Hants. One photo notes that Will Braden is the Officer Commanding (O.C.), and he is standing next to a vehicle with his Adjutant. On Sunday March 19th, Will was in attendance at White City Stadium, where two football games were played between soldiers of the Canadian Army and the American Army. In the morning game, called the 'Tea Bowl', the Canadians won 16-6, while in the afternoon contest, called the 'Coffee Bowl', the American shut out their opponents 18-0. Rules for the day saw each half played by the rules of one of the participants, along with refereeing by officials from that country.(41)

Once again, changes in the military establishment led to a change in responsibilities for Bill Braden:

> In consequence of the disbandment of 1 Canadian Equipment Assembly Unit, under authority A.O. 82, a number of officers have become available for posting and it is now desired that authority be given to effect the cross postings detailed below: Major W.G. Braden O.C. M.T. Inspectorate…w.e.f. 15 May 44 on posting to 1 Cdn B Vehicle Inspectorate (Overseas) R.C.E.M.E. (authorized under A.O. 87) and to be O.C.(42)

Bill Braden's 1944 Desk Diary gives some insight into the busy nature of his days in command. For example, on Sunday July 23rd, Braden embarked from England on an L.S.T. for the Continent, and two days later, he disembarked in France, to join the Canadian Army as it marched towards Germany.. On the 26th of July, he visited the town of Caen. He had his photo taken in the cemetery at Dieppe.

Major W.G. Braden pays his respects at the Canadian War Cemetery at Dieppe on 10 September 1944.

On 20 September, he got to visit Vimy and Arras. On 27 September, he moved to near Ghent; and there is a small notation in his diary, noting the day 'Dad died'. On 11 October, it was noted that he moved 'near Antwerp'. From 6-9 December, he had a brief period of leave in Paris.(43)

In late November 1944, it was time to move on again, as the First Canadian Army recommended Bill Braden as suitable for employment at the Army Proving Ground in Ottawa. (44) An assessment of Major Braden was made by the Senior Advisor R.C.E.M.E. at Canadian Military Headquarters:

> He has been overseas for three years, and after a brief period with a field workshop, has been employed on inspection of MT, for the past two years as 2 i/c, and later, OC MT Inspectorate in the UK and NWE. Although this officer is young, his

experience is specialized and should be of...benefit to the Proving Ground. With the MT Inspectorate as it is now organized and functioning, Major Braden can be spared from the field. His opportunities for promotion or new employment overseas are strictly limited due to his specialized experience.(45)

Major Braden and other Canadian Army Officers @1944-1945.

As of January 1945, Major Braden was attached to the Ministry of Supply's Wheeled Vehicle Experimental Establishment at Pinehurst Barracks, at Farnborough, Hants. Once again, as in the past, he had a problem with finances, this time because of his locale:

At the present time, three R.C.E.M.E. Officers are attached to this Unit for periods of from three to four months....The writer is attached for rations and quarters only to C.A.S.C. R.U. As the meal hour at noon is too early, and due to the distance to travel, even by bicycle, it has been found necessary to obtain lunch at a hotel which is considerably nearer to the Unit. Will you please arrange that I can claim for meal allowance (6 lunches per week). (46)

In early March, National Defence HQ amended Major Braden's time at the W.V.E.E. from 15 January 1945 to 15 March 1945, instead of the previously designated 15 May 45. They also went on to ask that "it would be appreciated if you would arrange for his posting to No. 1 Cdn Repat. Depot to be as near as possible to within two or three days of the date of the next Canadian draft."(47) Major Braden was to report to 1 Cdn Repatriation Depot on 16 March 1945, to return to Canada.(48) He was TOS No. 2 Dist Depot as of 1 April 1945, and he went off on disembarkation leave from 13 April to 12 May 1945.(49) Because of his background and his training, Major Braden was recommended by the Canadian Army Overseas for employment at the Vehicle Proving Establishment at National Headquarters. He was to cover off a vacancy for a Major E.M.E. at their "B" Vehicle Test Section, and to complete their establishment.(50)

While working at the Vehicle Proving Establishment, where he was the Officer in command of "B" Vehicle Test Section, Bill Braden had visits to Washington (22-27 July 1945), Noranda, Quebec (30 July-1 August 1945), and Comox, British Columbia (11 August-13 September 1945).

Major Braden (2nd from left) and other officers and civilians
in Comox, British Columbia, 4 September 1945.

At the start of August, Braden applied for his discharge, to be effective as of 6 November 1945: "The reason for applying for discharge is my desire to return to the B. Greening Wire Co. Ltd., Hamilton, Ont. I have been there since leaving McGill University in 1937.(51) National Defence concurred, and after receiving pre-discharge leave from 1-7 November 1945, he was struck off service No. 1 VPE (NDHQ) effective 7 November 1945, and taken off service No. 2 District Depot, effective 8 November 1945.(52)

The picture of Joan and Billy (at age seven months) that Bill Braden carried
with him in the four years that he was on service overseas.

His Medical Board Proceedings prior to his discharge from the Army, gave a hint of medical problems that would plague him during his career as a speedboat driver, a decade later:

> Exam-Back-no visible deformity. No limitation of movement. Complains of some
> tenderness over his lumbar muscles. No disability. Left knee-no swelling. There

is some increase in infra patella fat. No limitation of movement. No points of tenderness. All ligaments intact. No muscle atrophy. No disability on present exam.

B.P. Syst 105 Dias 70. History-at age 5 or 6 in bed 3 months with 'kidney trouble'. Back pain in lumbar region for 6 months....No urinary symptoms....Kidneys not palpable....Pain is in sacro-spinati and appears as hyperextension. Chest, heart, abdomen, glandular and nervous systems are negative.

[He was told to] report to D.V.A. if symptoms have not disappeared at the end of 6 months.(53)

The Medical Officer gave this write-up about the 'history of present and past disability':

....No important illness or injury in Army except for an episode of ... left knee following a long walk Nov 44. The knee became stiff, painful and swollen for about 3 days after which the symptoms...[declined]rather dramatically after a fall on the knee. General health has been excellent in the Army. For the past two months, he has had...pain and tenderness in ersto-vertebral angles, particularly the left...worst at night in bed when he lies on his stomach. Because of a history of 'kidney trouble' in childhood, he is concerned about his kidneys....(54)

When interviewed by the Department of Veterans Affairs, two days prior to being taken off the Active Force, it was noted that in 1940-41, Bill took training as a pilot. Nowhere else in his military records nor in his personal papers was this ever again noted. It goes on to provide a short account of his service, training and duties:

Major in Electrical and mechanical engineers. 57 months service, 40 months overseas, 4 months in N.W. Europe. All service as officer. 6 months courses on vehicles, Fords, General Motors plants. 4 months maintenance and repair of vehicles, army workshop.

3 months, second in command, 34 months in command of mechanical transport unit. 3 months with Ministry of Supply, in charge of proving and testing mechanical transport. Balance of service in charge of vehicle testing at Headquarters, Ottawa. (55)

His Veterans Affairs Counsellor gave the following assessment of Major Braden based on what he had seen in interviewing him:

Major Braden is mature and agreeable. He appears self reliant and capable and has had business experience in civilian life which, he feels was of value to him in his military work. His duties were in connection with all types of army mechanical transport, and covered inspection, testing, adaptation, proving ground operations, maintenance and repair. He advanced from practical work in these lines to a staff appointment involving control and administration of transport and proving units. He will return to his former work, administration and executive duties in connection with the office and sales division of a manufacturing company in which his family has an interest. He does not anticipate any employment problems….(56)

He was placed on the Reserve Active Officers General List as of 12 November 1945. Having ceased to be on Active Service, he applied for payment of the War Service Gratuity. With a total qualifying service of 1726 days, of which 1244 days were for overseas service, he was eligible for the sum of $1379.46. (57) Because of his active service with the Army, Major Braden was able to wear the France and Germany Star, the Defence Medal, and the Canadian Volunteer Service Medal and Clasp.(58)

How did one of Bill Braden's colleagues describe Bill's war service? Ted Frost, an English colleague, described it in this fashion, years later, to Bill's third son, Norman: "By day, we trained people how to ride motorcycles. By night, we rode across the countryside ourselves…."(59)

Three cousins volunteer for war service in 1941: (l-r) Army Lieutenant W.G. Braden,
Navy Sub-Lieutenant Owen Greening and Army Lieutenant Harcourt Bull.

Will Braden was not the only family member who was serving his country in wartime. His younger sister, Margaret, who had married an American, was living in the United States, and serving with the Women's Army Auxiliary Corps of the United States Army. She was written up in the Phoenix newspaper when she signed up in January 1942, as she was the 100th W.A.C. from Arizona sworn in for service with the Army from that state: "Mrs. Scott, a world traveler, has spent a large part of her life in London, and left there in 1938. She was well known both in England and Canada as an aviatrix, and her knowledge and experience in various countries will stand her in good stead."(60) As well as Francis Farwell volunteering his advisory services to the government, the Farwell family placed a summer home they owned at Milford Bay, Ontario, at the disposal of the R.C.A.F. as a convalescent home for the treatment of casualties. Will's cousins Owen Greening and Harcourt Bull were also in uniform. There are a series of photographs in one of Will Braden's photo albums. It shows the three young cousins all preparing to go off to war. Owen Greening joined the R.C.N. and was in charge of a small anti-submarine vessel. Harcourt Bull also joined the Canadian Army, like Will Braden, and served at Canadian Military Headquarters overseas. Fortunately, all of them returned, safe in both mind and body to pick up their lives in postwar Canada. Owen Greening took up a position with the B. Greening Wire Company, as might be expected. Harcourt Bull would join Royal Securities in 1948, and commence a forty year career in the field of investments in the city of Hamilton.(61) Brother-in-law John McColl, and friends Dave Ambrose and Douglas Wigle were all in the R.C.A.F.

Bill Braden's brother-in-law, Flight-Lieutenant John McColl, R.C.A.F.

Chapter 4: Work and Play

Earlier in the text, it had been pointed out that Will Braden had a new stepfather-in-law, by the name of Francis Farwell. Farwell had been born in Nantic, Massachusetts in 1894. In the mid-1920s, he came to Canada, to become the first General Manager of Provincial Transport (a large bus company) in Montreal, as well as running a cab company. In July 1931, he moved to Hamilton, when he and some business associates formed the Canada Coach Lines Limited. Under his leadership, Canada Coach Lines was extended throughout the Niagara frontier and into western Ontario. Later on, the company came to expand even further, and linked Niagara Falls, Buffalo, Galt, Brantford, Simcoe, and Tillsonburg amongst other centers. In 1946, he bought the Hamilton Street Railway Company from Ontario Hydro; he and his associates announced their intention to fully modernize the railway within five years, getting rid of street cars and replacing them with trolley coaches as well as gasoline and diesel buses. (1)

In that same year, he offered a postwar job to Bill Braden, in effect not only being his stepfather-in-law, but his employer as well. As you gauge the tone of the letter, remember that he is talking to a 31 year old man, who had served almost five years overseas , and had reached the rank of Major in His Majesty's Canadian Army by the end of his wartime career:

> In merging the two companies, Canada Coach Lines, Limited and the Hamilton Street Railway, I am in immediate urgent need of a high class technical expert to act as an assistant to Mr. Abray, our Assistant General Manager-Mechanical.
>
> Based on your past experience, particularly in the Army, you will qualify for this job, and in my opinion, it represents the possibilities over the next ten years of advancement and high salary to an extent greater than you can secure in any other line of endeavor. True the work will be hard and the hours will be long for a few years, but the ultimate reward will be very great.

I would like very much to let the matter delay until September in order that after four or five years of concentrated hard work in the Army overseas, away from your family under difficult conditions you could at least have one summer's holidays, but unfortunately I must immediately commence merging our garages, accounting departments, and other branches of the business. This includes the organizing and operation of a new large garage that would handle all major overhauls and all major repairs of all motor coaches for both companies. It is this job under Mr. Abray's direction that I want you to undertake.

You have now reached the age and have accumulated responsibilities where in fairness to yourself, your wife and children, you must put away childish things and take on the responsibilities of a man. It is only in this way that you can retain the respect of your family and friends. It does not matter how much money you and your wife now have or how much you may ultimately acquire, your responsibilities to your family and society are clear cut and well defined, and in my humble opinion now is the time for you to face up to them. (Boldface is author's choice)

I would like you to be in my office, Friday morning, July 26th at 9:00 a.m. ready to go to work. At that time, I will settle the question with you of salary and other duties. Unfortunately I cannot give you any time off for at least a year.

I am sincere in my belief that it constitutes a really great opportunity for you. I am now fifty-two years old. I have only about eight or ten years left at which time I will be out of gas. I would like nothing better than to have things developed where ten years from now, you and Joan's brother, John McColl, will be able to take over the management of this business....(2)

A Hamilton Street Railway personnel list from January 7th, 1950, showed that the Company consisted of 521 employees. Under the Admin List, Braden was listed as the Assistant General Manager. He entered service with Canada Coach Lines as of 12 September 1946, and with the Hamilton Street Railway effective as of 1 January 1947. Ironically, Will's long time friend, Basil Southam was hired on in this same period as Chief Engineer, joining Canada Coach Lines on 26 October 1946, and the Street Railway on 1 November 1947.(3)

What was Bill Braden's job at the Street Railway Company?(4) One of his duties was dealing with bus charters for schools and groups. As the school year of 1950-1951 started, he wrote letters to the Hamilton area high school Principals advising them of the services the Company was willing to offer during the year:

We are looking forward to serving your school again this year with chartered buses to carry the players to and from the football fields....the buses must be used for public service after players have returned to the school and would ask you to please request them to keep the buses just as clean as they possibly can.(5)

When asked by the Steel Company of Canada for a daily charter for its general office staff to go to and from the office, Braden noted in response: "We will give you the same rate for a 40 passenger bus as we charge for the regular small 27 passenger bus....(6)

He was also called upon to respond in writing to concerns and complaints from the community. To wit, when the Business Men's Association was unhappy with traffic tie-ups caused by H.S.R. buses at the corners of Main and Parkdale: "....Thank you for your letter of September 5th drawing our attention to the traffic congestion at the corner of Main and Parkdale Avenues...."(7)

In his report to the General Manager regarding charters, Bill Braden's statistics show the costs of running a bus charter business sixty years ago. A 27 passenger bus cost $8 one way, $13 return, and $13 per hour; whereas a 36-40 passenger bus cost $12 one way, $19 return and $19 per hour. In 1949 some 72,096 passengers were carried on charter routes with 6531 miles being covered. In the first eight months of 1950, the numbers carried were 39,743 over 4068 miles.(8)

On 11 May 1951, Braden met with Mr. Stipe from the Hamilton Post Office regarding the contract that the Street Railway had in place with the Post Office to transport working postmen across the city each weekday.(9) One letter in a file speaks about the relationship Bill Braden had with the employees of the H.S.R. It reads: "....I wish to thank you very much for the many deeds of kindness given by you to my late father. He spoke of you often here, and held you in high regard".(10)

In September 1951, Will received another summons from Mr. Farwell, inviting him to his office once again. This letter had a little more relaxed tone to it, not being typed on Street Railway letterhead, but rather being personally scribed on Braebourne Farm [his home] notepaper :

Dear Will: Your responsibilities as Assistant General Manager of the Hamilton Street Railway are now further increased by your election as a Director of the Company. Please be in my office at eleven a.m. next Tuesday Sept 11th. I wish to discuss your future increased duties and responsibilities with you. Francis.(11)

So in a five year period, Will Braden advanced from Assistant to the Assistant General Manager –Mechanical to Assistant General Manager of the Operating Departments of the Street Railway Company. He was a natural for a high profile position like this, with his dashing good looks, and his ability to deal effectively with people. He acted as a liaison with other bus companies. For example, the Sandwich, Windsor and Amherstburg bus lines in Windsor, Ontario, enquired about the H.S.R. charter rates. In his response, Braden noted: "…we have just started giving special discounts to Churches and Sunday Schools on Sundays only".(12)

The January 14th, 1952, report by Braden to the management team illustrated a problem that has plagued bus companies in Canada for decades: "Mr. Braden stated that complaints had been received regarding the unsafe condition of bus stops caused by ice and snow. The matter would be referred to the Garage for attention.(13) In the meeting in early March, it was stated that "…Mr. Todd spoke of complaints which have been received from operators regarding the lack of inside cleaning in trolley coaches. Mr. Braden was asked to make enquiries…."(14) In April 1952, the <u>Hamilton Spectator</u> had a photograph of Bill Braden giving out awards to H.S.R. drivers who were being honored for 'accident free miles'. His words echo down the years to those of us who are more familiar with the perpetual squabbling of the Toronto Transit Commission with its unionized drivers: "We're in business, and the product we sell is a ride. Only with courtesy and safety can our drivers sell that product".(15) In June, the management meeting heard about activities that were literally taking money from the pockets of the Company:

> It was reported by Mr. Braden that a type of racket was being worked on trolley coaches with money being taken from operators pouches. Tests had shown it was possible to extract money from the pouches and in one case recently, a senior operator had caught a boy red handed, and turned him over to the police….If a satisfactory means of solving the matter was approved, Mr. Todd instructed that an order be prepared by Mr. Braden notifying the drivers that they must follow the policy laid down by the Company of placing their pouches on the hook, wherever it was located….Mr. Todd said he wanted to see a copy of the order before it was placed on the boards.(16)

In the final meeting of June: "…the General Manager…wishes that Mr. Braden and Mr. Southam obtain drawings of available garage floor space at the Hamilton Street Railway and Canada Coach properties for the next meeting."(17) In late October discussion raged over paper transfers from one bus to another, and Will was appointed to a sub-committee of four members that had to table a report by the end of November. He reported to the Management Committee:

> ….that during the Safety Meetings held in October, operators present had discussed the transfer problem and felt that transfer points should be clearly marked for the benefit of the public and themselves. It was agreed that a tentative list [of transfer points] could be prepared for discussion.(18)

In a November meeting, Braden stated that a report had been received that H.S.R. inspectors' voices were being heard locally on TV programs.(19) In late November, he reported that some bus operators, after reporting in to the dispatcher, were going to the canteen to grab a snack, making themselves late for their run. Mr. Todd stated that a notice should be posted that drivers were not supposed to be doing this, under the promise of discipline.(20)

In early December, Will brought up an issue that was based on his own expertise with engines in the boat racing world. The Minutes noted that "Mr. Braden brought up the question of increasing the power in the Ford V-8's by making some mechanical changes, having to do with the crankshaft, and the pistons. It was thought advisable [by the Management Committee] to make an experiment with one engine." On a different note, one week later, he recommended that frames be made and located in the Ford buses, behind the driver in order that company notices might be posted [and be visible to the riders].(21)

The year 1953 saw a variety of issues come before the Committee that Mr. Braden was asked to do research/report on. On 5 January, he was asked to "enquire as to the reason for diesel buses 301, 305, 307 being in the yard at a time when all buses of this type were required to be operating in the basic service. It was to be understood that diesels were to be used in preference to gas buses in view of the difference in the cost of operating….(22) The next meeting had further demands. "It had been decided, Mr. Braden said, to have decalcomania signs posted in buses relating to the conduct of passengers. Decals with information relating to the fare structure would be posted in buses, commencing with Friday night January 16th….Mr. Todd asked the Committee on Transfers to move without delay to make its report. Mr. Braden said that Mr. McCulloch was writing to Winnipeg to ask for a copy of the new transfer, which he understood was to have gone into effect at the beginning of this year. Mr. Smith had prepared a list of transfer points….Mr. Braden was given permission to make enquiries as to the possibility of installing air conditioning ducts to tie up with the present system, in order that the two offices on the first floor, tenanted by the Personnel Department and the Superintendent of Operations [Mr. Braden] might be made more livable during the summer period of oppressive heat.(23) The meeting on 26 January, brought up several topics that were of a more serious nature:

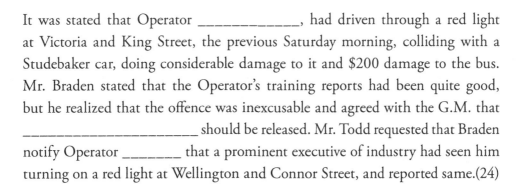

It was stated that Operator _____, had driven through a red light at Victoria and King Street, the previous Saturday morning, colliding with a Studebaker car, doing considerable damage to it and $200 damage to the bus. Mr. Braden stated that the Operator's training reports had been quite good, but he realized that the offence was inexcusable and agreed with the G.M. that _____ should be released. Mr. Todd requested that Braden notify Operator _____ that a prominent executive of industry had seen him turning on a red light at Wellington and Connor Street, and reported same.(24)

In February, the questions continued to be raised. When Mr. Braden enquired about the installation of a Mercury motor in a Ford bus, he was told that Mr. Farwell had requested that the action be deferred.(25) The big discussion of the month was the proposed shift from a six day week to a five day week for salaried workers:

> Mr. Todd asked Mr. Braden and Mr. Little to work out the details and present a report during this week in order that the change might go into effect the following Monday....It was to be understood that the switchboard would be open each Saturday and that a representative of the management group would be on duty each Saturday morning rotating on the basis of weekly shifts in the following order: Messrs. Little, Cooke, Braden and McCulloch.(26)

Bill Braden helped write a memo with the Comptroller to the General Manager, the following week, noting that:

> Effective Monday February 9th, 1953, the following will be the hours of work for the office staff, generally Monday through Friday 8:30 a.m. to 12:00 p.m. and 1:00 p.m. to 5:00 p.m., giving a one hour lunch period, with the exception of the switchboard, switchboard relief, and research department.

> ....Effective Saturday February 14h, and each subsequent Saturday, one representative of management and one switchboard operator-typist will be on duty from 8:30 a.m. to 12:00 p.m.

> ....It is considered that the essential work to be performed on Saturday morning in the main office will consist chiefly of typing up accident reports, typing of urgent letters, acceptance of telephone messages and public inquiries, handling of such emergencies as cannot wait till Monday morning, the disposition or reporting of unusual incidents, fire, fatalities etc., and much other duties as may arise....The management representative on weekend duty will <u>NOT</u> leave the city on Saturday or Sunday and will leave the telephone number at which he is available, with the Inspectors Office.(27)

In the meeting of 9 February, Mr. Braden "...requested that in future, there be avoidance of the mention of five day [work] weeks in advertisements appearing in the newspaper, in the Help Wanted column".(28) Two issues came to the fore in the next meeting:

> Dissatisfaction was expressed over the matter of bus washing in that the Operating Department was sending out dirty buses on Saturdays and Sundays; and Messrs.

Pickard and Braden were asked to go into the matter.....It was announced that one new type of fare box had been purchased and replacements would be ordered as the old ones wore out. Messrs. Pickard, Braden and Richardson were to select the proper location.(29)

Ironically at the same meeting, after weeks of study, it was noted that the cost to air condition the two main floor offices, including Bill Braden's, was to be $878.

It was not until May that Mr. Braden's name again appeared in the Minutes:

Mr. Todd noted that five spare men had been late last Friday, and three Operators had reported off sick. This together with the fact that there had been several resignations prompted him to suggest that Mr. Braden enquire into the situation, particularly with regard to those listed as being ill. He said that Mr. Mottram had mentioned the need for more trolley coach operators, and suggested that Mr. Braden look into this and report to him.(30)

In the next meeting, the key issue was vandalism, and how to stop it:

Mr. Pickard reported that upholstery in the trolley coach rear seats on King-Barton and Cannon routes had been slashed by someone using a sharp knife or razor blade at the rate of one a day, for two weeks, with three occurrences, being reported on Friday May 8....Mr. Braden was asked to have the operators check their coaches at the end of the line at each trip in an effort to fix the time of day when the damage was done.(31)

In early June, a summer time issue came to the fore: ....with regard to summer weight uniforms for operators in 1954, Mr. Todd said that the difficulties in the way were of such a nature to make such a step impractical, and requested Mr. Braden to so notify the Union Committee. (32) Later in the month, a disciplinary issue raised hackles at the meeting:

....When Mr. Braden reported that Mr. Mottram, Chief Dispatcher, had complained that operators were parking in the yard on payday, thus blocking the exit for trolley coaches, Mr. Todd said that notice should be given, warning against the practice, and that such warning should be enforced. When Mr. Braden also reported that one operator had said to Mr. Mottram 'Let Mr. Todd tell me', Mr. Todd picked up the telephone and instructed Mr. Mottram that henceforth any operators giving him impertinence were to be detained, and Mr. Todd sent for , in order that he might deal with them personally.(33)

The next meeting saw another disciplinary issue brought to the fore:

> Mr. Todd said that he had noted that there was a tendency on the part of staff members to take 1 ½ hours for lunch, instead of one hour, and that this must stop. It had been understood , he stated, when the five day week had been approved that the privilege would entail shortening the noon hour lunch period. Department Heads were to remind their staff that they were not to take more than the time allotted.(34)

In September, the Street Railway was going to do a promotion with Robinson's Department Store:

> Mr. Todd said that on Wednesday September 30th, Robinson's store would be holding its annual sale. Arrangements had been made for Operators to hand each passenger, between 9:30 a.m. and 3:00 p.m. a voucher printed and supplied the store, which would entitle the holder to two bus tickets if he presented the voucher with the sales slip to store officials. He asked Mr. Braden and Mr. Smith to attend to details affecting their departments.(35)

In November, the thoughts of the drivers and the managers turned to winter: "Mr. Braden reported that many operators complained about smooth [bald] tires and the resulting loss of traction in the snow….Mr. Todd asked Mr. Braden to secure permission to use the service station at the northeast corner of Gage and Mohawk for a bus loop as long as possible".(36) The following week, it was something completely different that was asked:

> Mr. Todd asked Mr. Braden to prepare a list of all the delegates that would be attending the fall meeting of the Canadian Transit Association in Ottawa, and to make all the necessary arrangements regarding trains and hotel reservations etc….Mr.. Todd asked Mr. Braden to check with the inspectors on point duty at King and James to make sure that the telephone is kept locked when no one is there….(37)

In December, winter weather conditions were discussed:

> Mr. Todd reminded those on weekend duty, representing management, to watch changes in the weather, and Mr. Braden was asked to remind Inspectors on duty to take the necessary steps to keep trolley coaches running all night in the event of storms so that there would be no interruption of service due to iced wires.(38)

As 1954 rolled around, there was a change in expectation of what was asked of citizens riding on H.S.R. buses and trollies: "Mr. Braden asked that signs be printed, requesting passengers to deposit their own fares, and stating that it was contrary to Company Regulations for the Operator to do so, the sign to be placed in the frame at the back of the Operator and facing the passengers...."(39)

A March meeting promised attendance at an out of city conferences for Bill Braden: "It was decided to send Mr. Braden [and three other members of the Management Committee] at the cost of $50 each to attend the special meetings on case interviews and the administration of discipline which will be held at the end of the Canadian Transit Association's spring meetings in April".(40)

Safety factors dominated the next meeting:

> Instructions were that Mr. Braden, Mr. Todd...were to be informed of any unusual situation of this type [electrical power fed to trolley car routes to be cut off for a lengthy period of time due to a fire]....Mr. Todd requested Mr. Braden to give thought to having the power house pull the switch three times at fifteen second intervals as a warning to coach operators, to pull into the curb, free of traffic, because a power cut-off was impending.(41)

An August meeting saw another safety issue brought to the fore:

> Mr. Smith read to Mr. Todd an operating order, dated July 6th, 1954, and signed by W.G. Braden, which in effect notified operators that they were not to proceed over railway crossings against any automatic signal in operation, even on a watchman's direction. The only circumstances under which they could proceed was when there was no train at the crossing, and they were waved across either by a policeman or an H.S.R. Inspector.(42)

In October, Mr. Braden was asked to deal with a disciplinary issue:

> Mr. Todd stated that he had noted that of the men delegated to drive buses on loan to the T.T.C., because of the flood conditions, one of their number, _____, appeared anything but neat and tidy. He requested that Mr. Braden check with Chief Inspector _____, and have _____ called in for an interview.(43)

In November, there was another discussion regarding the action of the bus operators:

Mr. Todd instructed Mr. McCulloch that the policy in the future when operators were injured, or were involved with clashes with passengers, while endeavoring to collect fares, would be written a personal letter of commendation to be signed by Mr. Todd, or in his absence, Mr. Braden, or in the absence of both by Mr. McCulloch.(44)

In 1955, there was a concern once again about vandalism on city buses:

It was not regarded as feasible to place receptacles for 'Take One' pamphlets near the rear doors because such action might invite juveniles to take out the pamphlets and scatter them around the vehicle. Mr. Braden drew attention to the awkward position of receptacles in Fords [buses] where the box was concealed by the handrail….(45)

Later in the month, Operators came up in two different meetings: "Mr. Braden said that prior to starting a drive on operator uniforms and appearance, a check should be made on the supervisory staff with regards to uniforms, coats etc. (46) The following week, "Mr. Todd expressed the desire that the word 'supervisor' or 'inspector' should appear more prominently on caps. Mr. Braden was asked to think about it".(47)

In May 1955, the topic of uniforms was discussed again:

….Mr. Braden acting on a report from Supervisor McKay suggested that some uniformed person be present on the loading platform of the Niagara Falls terminal at all times in order to answer the many questions. At present, information cannot be obtained at the times Mr. Shornholdts is on the platform, as he does not wear a uniform and people do not recognize him as a source of information….(48)

As the year 1956 rolled around, a variety of issues came forth to the attention of the Management Committee: "….It was stated that the new GM buses in the new paint scheme of cream and green would be delivered this week. Mr. Braden and Mr. Pickard will work out the arrangements with regard to the drivers…."(49)

A statement of policy came out in March that affected the responsibilities of Bill Braden: "The Operating Department of both the city and suburban companies are to be considered as one entity, under the direction of Mr. W.G. Braden". (50)

Vandalism of buses was a key discussion point at a meeting that same month:

….Mr. Pickard stated that the upholstery of buses was being ripped by vandals to the point that it was getting serious. Mr. Todd said that Mr. Braden and

Mr. McCulloch should consult as to the posting of a bulletin to all operators requesting them to make an inspection of the seats at the end of the line....(51)

A new proposed organization chart [dated 28 May 1956] drawn up by Mr. Braden and Mr. McColl at the request of Mr. Farwell was submitted for approval. It was felt that as an organization of more than 700 employees, there was adequate work and responsibility to be shared by two Assistant General Managers. The Operations end of the business would be the direct responsibility of Mr. Braden and the remaining operation of the business to be the particular responsibility of Mr. McColl. However, the two Assistant General Managers were to cooperate and share their total responsibilities at all times. It is in no way intended by us that any responsibilities or Company direction be taken from the General Manager but rather that he be given additional assistance in many matters pertaining to departmental function and responsibilities....The actual organization is ten men, each of whom is in charge of separate functions and each reporting to one General Manager. In addition, there are three more that have strictly staff responsibilities. Such breadth of control and responsibility mean strong, individual department leadership as well as excellent horizontal communication between department heads, or failing this cooperation, a resultant lack of communication between department heads and therefore a breakdown in organization. From observation, there are examples of both these characteristics in the actual organization as it stands today. There exists today a very cooperative and informal inter-departmental line of communication between Messrs. Braden, McCulloch, Pickard and Smith.

The proposed new organization chart reduces the spread of the number of people reporting directly to the General Manager from twelve to four, and places the responsibility of Operations for both H.S.R. and C.C.L. directly and entirely in the hands of Mr. Braden, together with the Traffic Department which includes the management of 'terminals'....Also this places Mr. Braden in the position where his operating staff practices can be felt throughout the Niagara Falls and Galt divisions....You have asked that we prepare an organizational chart for 1963 showing who will be managing the Company at that time in the absence of Mr. Todd. This was to be done so that Mr. Todd could commence training either Mr. Braden or Mr. McColl or both in the fields of corporate finance, banking and other higher policy matters.

In order that these two will gain more experience and assume more responsibility, it is necessary for them to be given an immediate position of more authority. The proposed new Organization Chart sets up both of us on an important level, and at present there exists between us a high degree of cooperation and communication. Thus the organization should currently become more effective and both of us through actual performance of these jobs should be able to learn enough and progress to the point whereby in 1963, either one or the other or both, could take over the job of General Manager. [Signed by both Bill Braden and John McColl] (52)

The proposed changes to the Street Railway's administrative organization did not meet with the approval of the owner:

> Dear Mr. Braden: Your letter to Mr. Todd, dated May 10, with a copy to me, is returned herewith, together with Mr. McColl's copy which I have secured from him. Several months ago, I approved an organization chart presented to me by Mr. Todd which pertained to both Canada Coach Lines and Hamilton Street Railway. Your letter does not conform to the proper organization procedure. Please discuss this question with Mr. Todd. He will outline to you my views with respect to the proper channels of responsibility and authority. Very truly yours, Francis Farwell, President.(53)

Later in the year, the Street Railway had to respond to demands placed upon it by the creation of a number of one way streets created in the city:

> Mr. Todd acquainted the Committee with details regarding the publicizing of the one way street programme, which would become effective October 28th. He also referred to the H.S.R. publicly in connection with route changes made necessary by one way streets. In this connection, he said that a folder would be distributed at main loading points on Friday October 26th by a staff recruited from former employee ranks and present operating establishment. The folder would contain individual maps indicating the changes in routes. It was left to Mr. Braden and Mr. McCulloch to decide on who would distribute the folders.(54)

In 1957, the question of a revised organization chart again came to the fore:

> In order to draw up a revised Organization Chart, it is necessary that each person write his own job description and the name of the person to whom he directly reports. Please prepare in considerable detail your present responsibilities. This is in order to clarify the various duties and responsibilities now being carried out by each one of us.(55)

The new organizational set-up went into effect before the end of the year, and Brigadier Todd had some final thoughts on it:

> ….charts of the organization controlling the Canada Coach Lines and the Hamilton Street Railway, with effect from December 3, 1957….I would be glad if all concerned would govern themselves accordingly and endeavor now to report up through the proper channels.(56)

The last thing Bill Braden did for the H.S.R. prior to his death was to help set up the Sarnia Transit Company, which was owned by Francis Farwell. The City of Sarnia had been without any public passenger transportation system since 16 July 1958. Sarnia City Council had decided to reduce the monthly subsidy to Cities Bus Service Ltd., from $6750 to $4097 per month. With such a decrease, the Company felt it could no longer operate, and closed down its service. Sarnia City Clerk G.A.M. Thomas had written to Brigadier Todd on 22 July saying: "City Council feels that it would like to obtain a new operator or firm to operate this important service. A proposition from you or your firm, if interested, would be appreciated at the earliest possible date."(57) The response from the H.S.R. owner was favorable:

> ....I am to advise you that Mr. Francis Farwell of Hamilton, Ontario, and his associates are prepared to form a Company to be known as 'The Sarnia Transit Company Limited' to operate a city bus service in the city of Sarnia, on or before the 30th day of August next. Funds will be made to the Company to the extent of $400,000. Contingent upon authority being received from the OMB, the City of Sarnia is to grant to the Sarnia Transit Company Ltd., a franchise to operate an exclusive bus service on the city streets for a period of ten years.(58)

Less than two weeks later. Mr. Todd wrote once again to the Mayor:

> Through no fault of our own, there has now been no bus service in Sarnia for a matter of four weeks, nor will it be physically possible for us to commence a service prior to 1 September. This means that the city will have been @seven weeks without a bus service; and the temporary impact of this on riding habits is hard to forecast. We do not believe that we can make either the equipment or the staff available in less than three weeks and in our opinion, it is imperative that service be restored coincident with the opening of the schools on 2 September next. Otherwise the repercussions would be very serious indeed. Under these difficult circumstances, we are prepared to establish a service and operate it as efficiently and economically as we know how.(59)

The final piece of correspondence about Sarnia Transit that has survived for over five decades is a memo from Bill Braden on 'things to be done prior to the commencement of service on 2 September 1958'. They included: "Garage facilities-adjacent land if possible for parking and spare parts room. Establish current account-Bank of Nova Scotia (signature cards). Postal address-P.O. Box or Garage-street and number."(60)

Frank Cooke was Superintendent of Operations at the time of Bill Braden's passing, and went on to take over Bill's job of Assistant General Manager (Operations) before ultimately becoming the General Manager of the H.S.R. He recounts what it was like to be on the Management Co-Ordinating Committee with Bill Braden:

> We all grew old together. There was the camaraderie of guys who had served in the forces [in W.W. II]. He was a mild mannered fellow, who never got overbearing. He was never blustery, and was easy to get along with. He treated people well, and was easy to work with and work for. He played the piano: he was not just a crazy guy who jumped off buildings and thought he was Superman. He was very amiable and liked to joke. He was not a stuffy, stodgy sort of person.(61)

A pick-up hockey game in the 1950s, and Bill Braden is quite visible
(2nd from left in the back row) wearing his Le Rosey hockey jersey.

In the 1940s, Will Braden took up motorcycle racing. This was a logical step considering he had motored across Europe at age 20; and had owned a motorcycle since his teenage years. For example, there was a 1947 newspaper clipping describing the 8th Annual Mud Run of the Blackhawk Motorcycle of Hamilton, which featured bike entries from London to Oshawa: "The Waterdown club's entry, Braden, was the outstanding performer of the day, riding like a veteran, despite the fact he had only seven miles on his own machine…."(62) A 1948 letter from Mr. H.R. Taylor from Taylor Matterson Limited, who were Auto & Motor Cycle Agents in England , gives some indication of the relationships that Bill Braden cultivated in the motorcycle community while overseas:

> I note that you and Basil [Southam] have apparently got these 350 AJS's and I can guess that you have well and truly cut and shunted them. I often think of the happy days we all had together and only wish that it was possible for us to again meet and have a really good 'bash', but still I suppose we must be content to just remember the happy times….With regards to your query re the new Trials machine, this is a really good job, and they have lightened it down considerably, shortened the frame, and believe me, it really handles.(63)

In the spring of 1955, he entered the Spring Motorcycle Trial. Racing for the Bill Braden Trophy, which he had donated to the race organizers. He did not win, but attained a second place in the second heat. On 3 October 1955, at a motorcycle scramble, riding smaller 200 cc bikes, Will Braden came second to his nephew George Marshall. In the 1955 Fall Motorcycle Trials, he did not come in the top three finishers. In the 1956 Mud Run, he finished first in the Visitors Category, besting his sixteen year old son, Bill, who came in second place. In the 1957 Spring Trials, Will ended third, losing out to George Marshall, but again defeating his son, Bill, who came in fifth.

If it was not racing bikes, or boats, it was a return to his youth and riding horses. In 1956, he bought a horse trailer, and picked up two horses, named 'Honey' and 'Fairfax', and began riding them after almost a thirty year hiatus away from horses.

It was an on-going battle between cars and motor bikes and boats for supremacy in Bill's heart. Even being at his house, Will was never far removed from his boat. The implement shed became a boat house, which could accommodate three boats. Instead it housed a boat, a jeep and a tractor. There was a workshop in the garage, as well as a light workshop adjacent to the house, which often accommodated one car and a boat.

Bill Braden on his motorcycle at his house in 1954

As a child, Gwyn Braden remembered her Dad as 'an avid reader'. He pored over books and magazines that had information about land and water speedsters, and had a file in his personal papers entitled: "W.G. Braden: Cars, Boats, Motorcycles: List of Books, Magazines". He subscribed to 'The Autocar' (1935-1941, 1943-1945), 'Motor Sport' (1935-1941), 'Canadian Boating Magazine' (1938-at least 1944),' Motor Boating' (1938-1941), 'Yachting' (1938-1941), 'The Motor Cycle' (1931-1941, 1943-1944). He had a list of 50 books for motorists from 'The Autocar'. He had a scrapbook just on the life of Henry Ford, entitled 'Lives of the Great Designers'. He kept a file just on Allard Special cars, noting showroom addresses and phone numbers, factory addresses and phone numbers, owners: with the type of Allard, phone and details, and the photographer who had taken pictures of Allard cars. He had a similar file for USA Briggs cars, noting the body, chassis, engine and description for each one. As well, Bill was a member of the following automobile clubs, and would be reading their literature: the B.E.M.C., the C.M.A., the B.M.C., the Royal Automobile Club (1934-1935, 1942 onwards), The Automobile Association (1934-1935), the Victoria Yacht

Club (1939-1940), the Muskoka Lakes Association (1939), and the America Power Boat Association (1939-1940). By the early 1950s, 'Sea and Spray' became the required reading, and there were notes and underlining about each of the boats for sale monthly, as Braden contemplated purchasing a new boat. There was also Speed Age (America's first motor racing magazine), as well as the A.P.B.A.'s 'Propeller', with its swap shop which featured hand written notes. There are two different scrap books of interest: one shows a variety of newspaper clippings from the 1955 Gold Cup in Seattle, where Bill Braden had driven **Miss Cadillac**, with emphasis on coverage of the race by the Seattle media; while the second scrapbook featured Donald Campbell and his **Bluebird** reaching the record speed of 202 m.p.h. There was also a file on sales books from Rolls Royce regarding their Griffon 57 Aero Engine; Derwent Turbo Jet Aero Engines, along with the Merlin 620 and 720 Series Aero-Engines. Each sales book came complete with a full color centerfold of the engine as well as performance sheets. Rolls Royce engines would play a key part in the **Miss Supertest** story. The file compared the output of different engines, what horsepower could be attained with each motor, and provided schematic diagrams of each type of engine.

Prize Day at Hillcrest in October 1952, and Chairman of the Board of Governors,
Bill Braden, accompanied by his wife, Joan, chat with two other Hillfield parents.

From 1951-1953, Will was the Chairman of the Board of Governors at Hillfield School in Hamilton. As noted in the school yearbook, the <u>Boar</u>: "The same **Bill Braden**, in addition to winning the above-mentioned honors in speedboat racing, was elected Chairman of the Hillfield Board of Governors at the recent annual meeting. We are especially glad to have Bill Braden as chairman, in that he is the first Old Boy to have been thus honored."(64) He gave the opening address on Prize Day on 31 October 1952, and his comments were about the administration of the School:

> He explained…the Board of Governors consists of sixteen members, elected for a four year term by the Corporation, together with a representative of the Old Boys Association. Its principal functions are to lay down the fundamental policies of the School, and meet the annual budget. The fees at Hillfield are the lowest of any comparable school in Ontario, but the staff salaries are not as high, nor is there a pension plan in operation. The Board is seeking means to provide a greater security for the staff.…Mr. Braden paid tribute to the work of Mr. Page, for the greatly increased enrolment, and the many innovations and successes that he had fostered, and to Mrs. Page 'for her really outstanding work and interest in the School.'(65)

In keeping with his interest in the sports activities around the School, at the end of the boxing tournament, Bill Braden presented the winners with their 'silver spoons' and the runners-up with 'bronze medals.' On Games Day on 4 June 1952, Joan Braden presented the winners with their prizes. On Prize Day 1953, <u>the Boar</u> noted:

> There were others for whose help and encouragement Mr. Page paid tribute. Amongst these are the Chairman of the Board of Governors whose two year term of office regrettably ends this fall, Mrs. Braden, and all members of the Board.…. Mr. W.G. Braden, Chairman of the Board of Governors, expressed his thanks to the members of the Board for their assistance during the year, and praised the work of the Headmaster and Mrs. Page, under whose guidance the School continues to grow.(66)

Once again, for the 1953 boxing season, Mr. Braden handed out the spoons and medals, which he and his wife helped to finance and donate to the School. Newspaper photographs show him and Joan in attendance at various activities on campus, especially Sports Day. Bill Jr. remembered those days and noted: "He would attend every running activity if his kids were involved. He attended because that was a competitive sport, and he was into competitive sports". (67) One particularly poignant photo from 1947 in an album shows Joan waiting at the finish line for Bill Jr. to finish his potato sack race. These outdoor interests were reflected in the family photo albums that Will put together. Very few photos were posed in the house. The only 'posed' photos were taken of Joan holding the newest young Braden, as she sat on the front step of the house. Other than that, photos were of the kids and the family doing something together. Be it in the Muskokas, near a boat house or at the lake, or skiing as a group in the winter time, family athletics were a key component of Will's life.

In May 1956, Bill Braden, an Old Boy of Trinity College School, Port Hope, visited the
school on a weekend to see his second son, John, march with the Air Cadet Squadron.
From (l-r)Gwyneth Braden, Joan Braden, John Braden and Bill Braden.

After the 1956 Harmsworth race, Bill Braden was in pain, as the constant pounding of the boat had injured his back. To get back into shape, he returned to his 'first love': racing motorcycles. Bill Braden Jr. commented: "The enthusiasm was there, though the physical conditioning was not...." (68) He also remembers his Dad taking the family on a trip to Switzerland in 1957. It was very rare for the family to go away, since Dad was either driving **Miss Supertest**, or he had **Ariel** out on the Ontario race circuit. He said:

> [the trip] seemed to have a plan of its own. In retrospect, he needed help in
> England to get the establishment to buy into allowing the Duke of York Trophy

Race to be held in Canada…..it was the first time we had spent time together as a family….summers had been influenced by boat racing.

…everywhere we went, he had already been. We visited two motorcycle shops in Birmingham and Manchester. We went to a Grand Prix race in Aintree. It was a repeat of what he had done {in 1935]. We went to the Old Boys Day. He tried to get a soccer game going. In Switzerland, we had to spend a day representing Canada regarding the Duke of York Trophy Race. We were introduced to the Duke of York organizers. The Duke of York race had never previously been held outside of England, but permission was given. We arrived somewhere and a new hydrofoil prototype was out on the water. We were given a ride on the hydrofoil. Mom was concerned that this was actually not a family holiday….

We went to a horse race track, a car track in France, and we stopped at an inn to see the woman who ran it. Every stop had some significance. It was not selfish but the whole thing did not make sense. A pre-planned itinerary was being marketed as a family holiday with various interests: we had to go to Versailles, the track at Nice: it would all fit the mold. We had lots to cover: every place we went there was a full itinerary. (69)

Chapter 5: Racing the **Ariel** boats

Pre- World War II Boat Racing

Bill Braden's first race boat was the **Ariel I** named after the English-made motorcycle, which he had driven and which had captured his heart. After its purchase in 1938, he competed in local races on Hamilton Bay. When he started racing, boat racing had a minimal stature in society. Except for Gar Wood, a few years earlier, having a boat to race was a bit of an accomplishment in itself. It was not like you could go down to the corner store and purchase one from its stock.

From his own notes, we know that Bill was involved in the Puslinch Lake Regatta in July 1940. It is stated that he was second in the first heat of 225 class, Division B, and first in the second heat. There is the briefest of mentions: 'took Dad for ride'. (1) It would have been interesting to have been able to read the father's mind, knowing as he did that racing was in the family genes, having himself served on several occasions as a mechanic to Harry Greening; but on the other hand, worried for his son's safety as he skimmed over water, at speeds far in excess to what automobiles were doing on the roads of the country. A letter survives from that July on Norman Braden's letterhead at Westinghouse, bearing the usual fatherly admonishments: "I hope you got up to Muskoka with the boat without any serious trouble, and that you will have an enjoyable and restful vacation, and not be too strenuous, but have a thoroughly enjoyable time. And then in the end, just to show that he was not 'too' angry, he closed with: "….my love to Joan, as well as to yourself. Affectionately yours, Dad". (2) A second letter, written in a similar vein, was forthcoming six days later:

> You certainly stole a march on your Dad by making the trip to Valleyfield, Quebec, with your boat, which I learned of from your Uncle Harry, who was anxious to know how you made out at the races, but I was unable to enlighten him on that score—in fact it gave me quite a surprise to know you had gone down there! I certainly hope you did well and had no serious trouble….

ARIEL I   1940

Bill Braden standing in the cockpit of Ariel I in 1940.

But once again, all was forgiven by the end of the page: "With much love to both Joan and yourself, I remain, Affectionately, Dad". (3)

Later in the year, he won the Quebec championship, and then piloted the boat to the Canadian championship for 225 class boats at the C.N.E. At the end of the racing season, there started a hiatus in Bill Braden's boat racing career that would last until he came home at war's end. Gasoline became rationed for the war effort, and boat design turned towards taking the hulls and putting powerful engines in them, and using them as motor torpedo boats (M.T.B.'s) to attack German seaborne trade.

1946 Boat Racing Season

After the war, Bill Braden's interest in cars diminished, and was replaced by an interest in speedboats and racing them.

In the postwar period, there were not a lot of aircraft motors available. No unlimited class speedboats were utilizing aircraft motors prior to 1948-1949. Before that day, owners and drivers were utilizing whatever engines they could get their hands on.

After Bill Braden returned to Canada in 1945 and was demobilized, he became the first Canadian race boat driver to become a member of the American Inboard Boating Association. (4) In 1946, he won the Ohio State Racing Championship, sponsored by the Warren Boat Club, driving his 135 cubic inch class **Ariel III** to victory, representing the Royal Hamilton Yacht Club, over the waters of Mosquito Lake before a crowd of some 7000-8000 on shore. This was the feature event of the day, since the 225 class race was called off as Guy Lombardo was unable to get there in time, and there was only one other entry in that field. Some 150 boats and drivers had converged on the lake from eight different American states for the weekend's races (5). As well, Braden came in fourth in the United States National Championships at Red Bank, New Jersey, again in the cockpit of **Ariel III**.(6) These successes even merited him a mention in the Hamilton newspaper:

> Hamilton, it might be observed, has more than passing interest in the Gold Cup
> races this season, because one of the entrants is a Hamiltonian-William Braden.
> Mr. Braden is one of two Canadians who still pilot fast craft….experts give both
> a chance to finish bang up in the whirling water tests.(7)

The 1946 Gold Cup race in Detroit was the 39th running of the challenge, and featured its largest field ever entered, a total of 26 boats. It was the first time that it had been staged since the outbreak of war in December 1941, and was scheduled for Labor Day. The race was a total of 90 miles in length, consisting of three 30 mile heats. Before a crowd estimated at anywhere from 100,000 to 250,000 along the shores of the Detroit River, Bill Braden endured a bad day of racing, driving **Ariel II**. He received a D.N.F. in the first heat, when he was flagged off the course, being in eighth place out of a field of nine boats before one lap was completed, and trailing the leaders by more than ten minutes at the finish. **Miss Canada** had a similarly forgettable afternoon, blowing her supercharger, and stalling out in the sixth lap of a ten lap qualifying test. The only Canadian who met with any success on the afternoon was musician Guy Lombardo, driving **Tempo VI**, who won each of the three heats his boat entered, and averaged a record speed of 68.128 m.p.h. Using the same boat, Lombardo had won the race back in 1939, and added the cup to the National Championship he had won earlier in the summer at Red Bank.(8) Later in the summer, Braden had a fifth place finish in the fifteen mile Silver Cup race over the same waters.

1947 Boat Racing Season

In 1947, Braden put **Ariel II** into a large number of competitions, hoping for more success than had occurred during the previous racing season .The successes of the boat during this campaign were attributed to the wizardry of mechanic L.W. "Chic" Townshend of Hamilton, who had been tuning speedboat engines for three decades. Townsend was a story in his own right, owning a 1929 English made Sunbeam automobile that once was the personal property of Sir Henry Seagrave, and which had been given by him to Gar Wood in 1930. Townsend had made a number of alterations to the vehicle, so that in 1947, it would attain speeds of over 100 m.p.h.(9) He had been involved in tuning stock cars when Bill Braden came knocking on his door. Even when working around the boat, his attire was a shirt and tie.

Bill Braden watches his mechanic 'Chic' Townshend work on the engine of Ariel II @1947-1948. Note the white shirt, tie and vest: not exactly the attire one would expect to see on a mechanic.

In mid-July, Braden ended fifth to Robert Bogie's scarlet colored **Blitz II** (F-9) in the 225 cubic inch class, as Bogie captured the Belleville Sargent Gold Trophy, emblematic of the Belleville Rotary Club Regatta. The day's racing was also highlighted by the victory in the Class D Runabouts by Picton Mayor Harvey McFarland. (10)

Bill Braden sitting in the cockpit of Ariel II. Just like his mechanic, he is dressed in his Sunday best.

On 12-13 July 1947, Braden drove **Ariel II** in the forty-five mile Henry Ford Memorial Regatta: the first powerboat regatta sponsored by the Detroit Boat Club. The <u>Detroit News</u> described the weather conditions around the 7 litre class race:

> Detroit Boat Club, oldest rowing centre in America, held its first powerboat regatta on the Detroit River, Saturday. While crowds on the Detroit and Belle Isle shores hardly approximated the throngs that have witnessed Gold Cup and Harmsworth events, the spots of vantage on the two banks of the two and a half mile course all had occupants... There was no way of guessing the number present. The day was perfect. There were a few white clouds decorating the blue skies. The breeze was soft and upriver against the current and ruffling the surface

slightly, but the course was not choppy….Bill Braden…did 53.491 mph to win the first heat of the 225 Division One class. **Blitz II** was second and **Ballyhoo** third. Five boats started, two failing to finish. (11)

Ariel II sitting on her flatbed on which she was towed from race to race.

Braden won each of the three heats of five miles length, which meant two times around the 2 ½ mile course with heat speeds of 53.491 m.p.h., 55.849 m.p.h., and 55.174 m.p.h., to capture the Weyhing Trophy with 1200 points compared to **Blitz II**'s 825 points. He defeated Bob Bogie in **Blitz II,** who had been the 1946 Canadian Champion, as well as Gib Bradfield in **Buckeye Baby** (F-3), who had been the 1946 U.S. National Champion. The boats raced in a counter-clockwise direction, similar to the Gold Cup boats, but opposite to the direction of the Harmsworth Trophy competitors.

Braden went on to enter his boat in the major Gold Cup event, racing in the unlimited class heats, but did not get into the first heat on time, finishing second in each of the remaining heats. In the second heat, she defeated **Miss Great Lakes** (G-4), powered by a 12 cylinder Allison engine, which had been the favorite to win the trophy, but lost out to **Dukie** (G-9), owned by

Detroit tool shop owner 'Whitey' Hughes, who posted a winning speed of 57.783 m.p.h. In the final heat, next to the winner, **Miss Peps** (G-99), who had a speed of 47.332, Braden had the only boat that remained running out on the course. Winning driver Danny Foster put the day into perspective when he said at the end of the races: "It was a question of who could finish rather than how fast you'd go."(12) Had **Ariel** arrived at the first heat in time, and had she attained a second place there, she would have won the trophy based on total points.(13) As it was, **Miss Peps** pulled in 827 points, with **Dukie** garnering 800 points, and Braden attaining 600 points, to obtain a third place. Why would Braden drive his boat in a higher class against bigger competitors? On one hand, he hoped to pull off an upset. As well, it gave him more time in the water to test out the boat, and grow more familiar with the course, which would give him an advantage over the other drivers when it came time to race in his own class.

Braden moved on to attain a third place at Barrie on 2 August, and repeated the same success at Picton on 4 August, where his boat won the second heat.

On 30 August, there was the Silver Cup race on the Detroit River. The <u>Detroit News</u> article got confused, noting that **Ariel II** was driven by Bill Greening, and Braden himself penned some exclamation marks on the article in his scrapbook!

> ….In the first heat of the 225 race, Bogie has to fight off a challenge from Bill Greening in **Ariel II** which finished second. Bogie averaged 60.367 mph for the nine mile heat, which was three times around the so-called Gold Cup course. Only five boats survived for the second heat and **Ariel II** was the first over the line. It was a two boat race from the start with **Blitz** chasing **Ariel** until the last lap when Bogie put his **Blitz** ahead of **Ariel** on the backstretch, at the lower turn near the Belle Isle Bridge, and came on to win by 200 feet. **Blitz** averaged 62.168 mph in the second heat, and amassed 800 points to 600 for **Ariel**. (14)

The race for the Edenburn Trophy consisted of three heats of nine miles each over a three mile course. In that first heat, **Blitz II** won by .62 seconds and she repeated her win in Heat #2 by some 7.5 seconds. In the final heat, in a driving rainstorm that pelted the drivers with what felt like bee bee shots she triumphed by @34 seconds. Bogie's best heat speed was 62.329 m.p.h.; compared to Braden's 61.278 m.p.h. Braden was a close second to Bogie, but a second nevertheless.

Bill Braden trails Bob Bogie's Blitz II on the Detroit River in 1947 in search of the Edenburn Trophy

Ironically on the same weekend, Braden's friend and racing associate, Basil Southam was competing for the Tom Boyd Trophy, in the 225 cubic inch class, Division II; and attained a seventh place, through two seventh place finishes and a D.N.F.

On 1 September, racing in the 7 litre class, in quest of the Fageol Trophy and the American Sweepstakes, over a three mile course, with each heat consisting of fifteen miles, Lou Fageol himself won the race in his boat **So Long.** But Fageol was self conscious about winning a trophy that he had donated himself, and had made an agreement with race organizers that if his boat came first, the second place boat would take home the hardware. And so, 'Wild Bill' Cantrell driving **Schafer Special** came to win the trophy. Cantrell set a record lap time for 7 litre boats in winning the final heat, with a recorded speed of 68.628 m.p.h. Once again, Robert Bogie in his **Blitz II** bested the Waterdown boat which came fourth, surpassing two Ohio based boats which did not start the final heat. Braden's best heat of the day was 63.668 m.p.h., some 3.4 seconds off of Fageol's best time. (15)

At the end of the summer, the boat placed third in her class at the Canadian Championships in Toronto, attaining the fastest heat of the day.

Bill Braden speeds by a crowd outside the Canadian National Exhibition in 1947.

1948 Boat Racing Season

The 1948 racing season saw more disappointing results than had occurred in the previous campaign....On 31 July, Hamilton hosted its first annual international inboard power boat regatta. As the <u>Hamilton Spectator</u> described the day:

> Hamilton's first annual international inboard power boat regatta was run off Saturday, and although weather conditions made havoc of the program, officials managed to finish off the event s before darkness closed down over the bay course.

> Scheduled to start at 1:30 p.m., the races were repeatedly postponed due to a 25 mile an hour wind which kicked up rough water. The thousands of fans who had

gathered along the bay front to witness the regatta became disappointed at the hourly postponements and slowly dwindled away.

...Drivers of the hydroplane craft had refused earlier to take their boats out as this type of boat is unable to race against any wind of more than 10 miles an hour. The first hydroplane event did not commence until 7:45 p.m. when the water had calmed down considerably....A boat light had to be put at the far turning buoy to enable the drivers to see where to turn....The course, a distance of one and two-thirds miles was circled three times by the drivers, which made up the required five miles.

The performance of Jack 'Pops' Cooper, of Kansas City, was the feature of the day as the veteran speedster, who is over 70 years of age, won both the 135 event and the 225, Division I event. When his 226 cubic inch craft proceeded to act up in its trial runs, Cooper brought out his 135 boat, **Tops Blue Blazer**, and raced in both the 225 and the 135 classes. In the first heat of the 225 race, Cooper came in second and in the next heat, he placed first to tie with Sid Street, who also had a first and a second. Cooper won the event on elapsed time, however, but was unable to win the trophy due to a regulation of the A.P.B.A. as he was racing a boat which was out of its class. It is quite a notable achievement in power boat racing to win the higher class event with a smaller boat. (16)

In the 225 cubic inch class Division 1, Sid Street in his **Z-Z-Zip** took home first place and the H.B. Greening Cup. Bill Braden who ended in second place, with a fastest lap speed of 58.2 m.p.h., won a tray donated by the <u>Hamilton Spectator</u>, and defeated Bob Bogie who came in third place.

This was followed up by a fourth place in the Picton Gold Cup, run on 2nd of August, again with a fastest heat of 61.5 m.p.h. More than for Braden's racing expertise, this day at Picton was remembered for the unfortunate death of Jack O. "Pops" Cooper, the white haired, bespectacled driver, who had started his career behind the wheel at age 48, driving outboard hydros, and switched to inboards at age 55. Over the next thirteen years, he had established many records in the 91, 135 and 225 cubic inch inboard classes. Prior to the 225 class race at Picton, his hydroplane had had ignition problems, so he chose to race against the larger boats in his smaller 135 cubic inch hydroplane. As described by witnesses:

Thousands of spectators witnessed the tragic accident that resulted in the death of Jack O. 'Pops' Cooper at the Regatta at Picton , August 2, 1948....The tragedy cast a spell of gloom over the events of the day. When the spectators saw and realized what had happened immediately before the official barge, a great gasp came from the crowd. This was followed by dead silence.

In the second heat of the 225 Gold Cup race, the boats beat the starting gun. All but William Brayden, in **Ariel II**, and John Bogie driving **Blitz II** were well across the starting line when the gun sounded. The boats were doing a terrific clip and before the signal of a false start could be given they were at the first turn. The red flag at the turn went up but the majority of drivers were swinging around the first buoy and they were out of line of vision at the warning flag. Coming into the homestretch, all boats were well-grouped. Cooper, on the inside, was driving at a record rate in his little 135 cubic inch boat.

….all the way up the stretch, "Pops" was just tipping the water with his prop and rudder every 500 feet. The boat was actually in the air when a light gust of wind swept under the craft and flipped it right over backwards….From the official barge the Cooper boat looked like a barn door swinging open. It all happened in seconds. The boat must have been doing 90 m.p.h. at the time. It gracefully took off in the air. The bow rose high into the air. The stern seemed balanced on the surf for a fraction of a second as the bow went on over to point in the opposite direction to which the craft had been travelling. "Pops" Cooper was thrown clear of the boat in a sitting position. As the bow of the tiny craft keeled over, it must have hit Mr. Cooper on the head. Parts of the boat flew in all directions. Cooper was lost in the debris and surf…. (17)

Cooper suffered multiple skull fractures, a cerebral hemorrhage, a broken shoulder, broken ribs and an injured pelvis. In a situation that would be eerily reproduced a decade later in Huntsville, Paul Sawyer, driving **Belligero** jumped into the water, and found Cooper face down, unconscious in the water. Sawyer held his face out of the water. Mr. and Mrs. Michael Steffen's boat was tied to the official barge, and they set out for the crash site. Bill Braden, in fourth place at the time, jumped into their boat and helped pull Cooper's body out of the water, so he could be taken for medical attention on shore. A sports writer had these observations: "Sportsmanship, as exemplified in the actions of….the Bradens and the Sawyers, leaves a clean, sweet taste in the mouth. Speedboat racing will never decline as long as gentlemen and sportsmen of the ilk of these men are at the wheels of powerful boats".(18) Nine days after the accident, "Pops" Cooper succumbed to his injuries in a Syracuse, New York hospital at age 68.

Racing at Detroit in the Silver Cup Regatta, Braden was in search of the Fageol Trophy, named after the unlimited driver, Lou Fageol, who, as noted earlier, had donated it. The three heat, 45 mile race saw winning driver, Dan Arena, in his boat **Will-o-the Wisp**, which had been

72

purchased on the Friday before the race from Dr. W.G. Robinson of New York (19) posted a 3rd, 2nd and a 1st in the heats to garner 925 points; while Bill Braden in his **Ariel** came second with 850 points, including a fastest heat of 64.9 m.p.h., ahead of Bill Stroh, in **Nuts N'Bolts** who finished third with 769 points. A penalty on the final heat cost Bill Braden the victory. **Ariel II** jumped the starter's gun, and was docked a penalty lap, which gave Arena the victory.(20) Ironically, old nemesis, Bob Bogie had posted a best lap speed of 63.303 m.p.h. in the first heat, but failed to show up for the second heat, having broken a piston rod. There was a second place in the chase of the Ederburn Trophy as well on the same weekend. At the season's end, **Ariel II** finished sixth in the Canadian Regional Championships in the 225 Division 1 class in Toronto. The boat had a speed of 57.1 m.p.h., and a D.N.F. in the second heat.

Bill Braden at the Gravenhurst Regatta in 1948.

1949 Boat Racing Season

In 1949, Braden's old boat **Ariel I** was in the news once again. The hull was owned at this time by Harry Luscombe, who owned and operated the Yellow Cab Company and Grafton Garage in Hamilton. The <u>Hamilton Spectator</u> had this report:

> **Ariel I**, an eighteen foot power boat whose world speed records have stood for a decade, exploded and burned to the waterline in Hamilton Harbor this morning, almost costing the life of its owner…who was hurled ten feet by the blast. Mr. Luscombe suffered burns and the boat was completely destroyed. The accident occurred at the Hamilton Power Boat Association docks immediately west of the Royal Hamilton Yacht Club. The explosion occurred when Mr. Luscombe turned the ignition switch on. Showered with debris and flaming gasoline, Mr. Luscombe leapt to his feet, beat out the flames and ran…to summon the fire department…. Firemen poured water into the boat, but only a few keel timbers remained intact, supporting the motor and drive shaft….(21)

Braden was racing **Ariel II** in all the stops on the racing circuit. On 3 July, in the Maple Leaf Regatta at Windsor, Braden finished third in the 225 cubic inch class. . In mid-July, the Kiwanis Club of Belleville held its first annual power boat regatta off Massassaga Point in the Bay of Quinte. The race was sanctioned by both the Canadian Boating Federation and the American Power Boat Association. In the 225 cubic inch class, Sid Street of Kansas City took top honors in his **Zip Zip** besting Bob Bogie, with **Ariel II** coming in third with 224 points. (22)

In the Ford Memorial race, she ended in fifth place after losing a propeller, and almost sinking. At the start of August at Picton Bay, the Gold Cup event was won by John Bogie driving his brother's **Blitz II,** with Bill Braden finishing second, and being the only other boat to finish the second heat of racing. Bob Bogie, driving his new **Blitz III** finished fifth.(23) In the Gold Cup competition, Bob Bogie and Bill Braden fought it out again, with Bogie defeating Braden by 3/10 of a second in the second heat of the race, to garner first place and the Gold Cup with a grand total of 569 points, overcoming his fourth place finish in the first heat.(24) In the Silver Cup Regatta at the end of the summer, Bill Braden won the Ederburn Trophy with his first place finish. The C.N.E. ten mile unlimited race had a bit of class with famed musician, Guy Lombardo racing his own boat **Tempo VI** to a victory. As reported in the <u>New York Times</u>:

> Hampered by the narrow course, inside the seawall, Guy Lombardo raced his **Tempo VI** with 225 class boats to win one heat and lose another in the ten mile unlimited race at the C.N.E. yesterday. Lombardo won the first heat outside the seawall at noon….Four hours later, Lombardo turned up straight from the big C.N.E. dance tent where his Royal Canadians are playing. In dress shoes and the

full dress he wears to lead his band, the bandsman-boatman climbed into **Tempo VI**. Rough water, which postponed the race from yesterday, was churning up again, and Lombardo gamely consented to run his Harmsworth class boat inside the seawall, where the 225 class boats would have protection. He was hampered on every turn…. (25)

Bill Braden came third in each of the heats in **Ariel II**, besting **Blitz II** in the second heat. Lombardo posted a first and a second, where he finished barely 200 yards behind Sid Street's **Z-Z-Zip** for the two heats, to capture the Canadian title on points.

1950 Boat Racing Season

Prior to the start of the 1950 racing season, Bill Braden received a thorough write up in the Hamilton Spectator:

> ….Back in the 1920s, Hamilton boasted one of the top speedboat drivers and designers of the day, Commodore Harry B. Greening. His success…put Hamilton on powerboat racing's map….Since Commodore Greening retired from competitive racing twenty years ago, Hamilton's fame as a speedboat centre slowly dwindled.

> A few years ago, however, his nephew Bill Braden, began to win attention both in Canada and the U.S. with his hydroplane boats **Ariel II** and **Ariel III.**

> Now Braden and two fellow members of the year old Hamilton Power Boat Association…have under construction two of the most modern types of hydroplanes ever designed. These craft are built from plans of three separate boats that presently own world's records in their own class.

> They are patterned on what is known as the 'California design', which means that they have a very lightweight hull. They are the first of their type ever to be built in Canada. Looking like huge water spiders, these boats are inboard powered streamlined craft that reach speeds close to 100 m.p.h. Sponsons, looking almost like wings, are built to the sides of the hull, and the boat rides on these two sponsons and the propeller, thus reducing water friction to a minimum.

> When hitting top speeds, the boat actually flies, with only the propeller remaining in the water.

All three boats are being built by Bob Thompson at Thompson's Boat Works. These new boats will raise the total of Hamilton-owned hydroplanes to seven, more than any other club in Canada can boast. Of the four which are presently in existence, however, only one, Bill Braden's **Ariel II**, has done much competitive racing.

The story of the building of these three new boats is actually the story of the Hamilton Power Boat Association. Formed a little more than a year ago in January 1949, the club has grown to such an extent that plans are presently under way to build a club house this spring on the property just west of the Hamilton Yacht Club.

There is currently a membership of 125, all of whom own boats, either inboards or outboards, which makes the club the largest in Canada. Last summer, the Hamilton Association staged its first regatta, which was limited to outboard motor boats. This year they plan to stage two, one outboard regatta on 29 July and an inboard regatta on 5 August. The latter is under the sanction of the American Power Boat association, and is included in the Canadian circuit of ten regattas. Points won in these sanctioned regattas all go towards the awarding of the coveted national championship trophies in the various classes.

The Canadian circuit is recognized as the toughest in North America and in past years American entries have been taking most of the prize monies back to the U.S. with them. Since the local association was formed, Braden has been working on several of his fellow members to build new hydroplanes.

The power in all three boats will be provided by Ford V-8 engines, which the owners will rebuild in their own workshops….By using such tricks as increasing the size of the intake ports and using a high lift cam, they will increase the revolutions per minute to 5,800 as compared to 3,600 for a stock engine.

Best known of the local drivers, and only one of the three builders who had previous experience with hydroplanes is Bill Braden. He is recognized in racing circles throughout North America as one of the smartest and cagiest men in the sport.

He has had a great deal of success with **Ariel II** and he hopes to do even greater things with his latest….Braden has been very successful in carrying on in the tradition of [Greening]

….His latest boat, which is presently being built, is designed after the **Belligero II**, the holder of the world's record of 99 m.p.h. for one mile, in the 225 Division I class.

…A power boat must be perfectly balanced, and it sometimes takes years to get the craft running to perfection. When a boat is not running as it should, the motor will be shifted to change the distribution of weight, or the propeller size will be changed. A boat is balanced for the driver, and will not give the same performance for a driver of different weight. It took Bill Braden four years to get **Ariel II** running right, but he is hoping that **Ariel IV** will be much better behaved. (26)

The year also saw Braden compete at Windsor where he sought to enter the Maple Leaf Regatta, but only obtained a D.N.S. because of mechanical issues. Moving to Detroit, the Canadian boat obtained a fourth place, with a Best Heat Speed of 55.1 m.p.h.

1951 Boat Racing Season

This year saw Bill Braden owning a new boat:

Although Braden has been racing hydroplanes for years and is recognized as one of the foremost drivers and owners in Canada, he has never stopped looking for a boat that could more than hold its own in any regatta in North America.

To say he found such a boat is a vast understatement for he is now the owner of the former **Belligero II**, the first 225 cu in craft in the world to ever hit 100 m.p.h. Renamed the **Ariel IV**, the boat is still the second fastest of its kind in the world. Braden bought the boat from Paul Sawyer, a Californian who sold it after his other craft of the same design; **Alter Ego** broke **Belligero**'s record with an amazing speed of 115 m.p.h.....

Powered by Mercury V-8 racing engines that generate 250 h.p., these boats ride on just two suspension points, thus reducing water friction to a minimum. These two points are situated on sponsons running down the side of the hull, and when the boat hits high speeds, daylight can be seen under the hull as even the top half of the propeller is clear of the water.

Methanol, a synthetic wood alcohol, which burns twice as fast as gasoline, is used to power Division I boats. Almost impossible to get in Canada, a year ago, methanol can now be obtained in small quantities.

It was just a quirk of fate that prevented Braden from getting his hands on **Alter Ego.** Last summer [1950] when Sawyer was here for the H.P.B.A.'s annual regatta, he had **Alter Ego** up for sale, and was racing **Belligero II,** then the world's record holder. Braden was very much interested in buying the craft, but import restrictions in effect at the time, made it impossible for him to bring it over the border….by the time he [Sawyer] got through, he had broken his own mark, and the boat was not for sale at any price. He then put **Belligero II** on the selling block and when the import restrictions were lifted early this year, Braden was not long in snapping it up.

What makes the story even more ironical is that Braden has just had a boat built to the exact specifications of **Belligero II.** Why then did he buy the original? That is a good question, but as power boaters will tell you, copying a record holder doesn't mean a thing in speedboat racing. When Sawyer owned **Belligero II,** he shifted his engine more than twenty times within a space of two inches before he found the balance at which the boat performed best. Although Braden wouldn't think of meddling with the balance of the boat, he did make one change when he purchased the craft. He had Bob Thompson remove the original sponsons and replace them with some of sturdier construction. All American boats of this type were built with what is known in the trade as 'California type hulls', which cannot stand the pounding of the rougher waters of Canadian lakes.

….Even with the heavier sponsons, Braden ran into trouble in rough water at the Gananoque Regatta recently. After placing third in the first heat, he was leading in the second [heat] when one of his sponsons ripped off and flew high over his head. He immediately headed for shore, and got his boat up before it sank, returning later for the flying sponson….He has had very few spills…not having experienced one since he owned **Ariel I** before the war.

He suffered a near disaster in Windsor several weeks back, however, when he raced his [new] craft for the first time. He was thrown out of his cockpit with great violence, landing on the deck of his craft, with one foot in the water. He managed to cling to the wheel however, and dragged himself back in. For the next week, he was black and blue from ankle to shoulder.

All hydroplanes are tough to handle at high speeds, but Braden finds his latest boat especially so. 'Boats of this kind actually fly at times as they leave the water entirely when they hit a swell at high speeds'.

The worst part of racing, according to Braden, is when you are forced to pass through the wake of another boat coming into contact with the roostertail, which the rival boat throws up. Caused by the top half of the propeller whirling around and hitting the surface of the water with terrific force, the plume shoots up in a semi circular arc, and although it appears quite harmless, it is exactly the opposite. It has the force of a fire hose, as can be testified by Braden, who had the peak of his sturdy crash helmet almost torn off by the power of the stream in a recent race.(27)

How had he come to own such a successful and famous boat? When **Alter Ego** became the better of the two boats, Sawyer said that he was willing to sell **Belligero,** and chose to sell it to Braden. It was purchased as a result of Canada Customs allowing some boats in under certain conditions (possibly a 'one only' entry). There were no known conditions to restrict the fact that the boat was imported, and was written up in several articles, including the one in the <u>Hamilton Spectator</u>. The date of import was late 1950 or early 1951. The name of the boat remained **Belligero** for a period of time.

Regarding **Ariel V**, the Government followed a much different import policy. Namely it was impossible to get an OK like with **Ariel IV**. It appears that a misleading and complicated plan was developed to get the boat into the country. American driver Bob Schroeder from Buffalo would deliver her to Shepherd Boats, where repairs would be effected on her. The boat, **Alter Ego**, was moved from there to a Hamilton shop where several other boats were being stored. An accumulation of leaves initiated a vacuuming up of debris in the boat storage area. The vacuum had an electrical arc, and Dad's new boat burned, leaving only the front half of it intact. I remember driving to Hamilton at @8:00 p.m. to see the burnt hull. The boat was subsequently moved to a location near Peterborough. (28)

There was a new face in the Braden camp for this racing season. Gil Zamprogna of Hamilton was the new mechanic taking care of the **Ariel** boats, starting a relationship that would endure up to the time of Bill Braden's passing in 1958. Zamprogna had been a mechanic at Wellington Motors (a Hamilton Ford dealership). **Ariel** had a Ford motor. Francis Farwell went to them and said: 'I want to hire your best mechanic' and on meeting with Zamprogna, hired him on the spot. Gil went to work at the Hamilton Street Railway, where the self-professed 'grease monkey' worked on their fleet of buses, as well as on Braden's race boats. Bill Braden Jr. recounted a story of Gil Zamprogna working on the boat while his Dad had it going full speed in the water. He noted that Zamprogna was holding on to the boat's deck with one hand, and making repairs with the other hand. (29)

Braden started the racing season at the end of June at the Maple Leaf Regatta in Windsor. The course was 1 2/3 miles in length, and in the two heats, **Ariel** ended fourth and third, to end the day in third place.

He next moved on to Valleyfield, Quebec, for what the <u>New York Times</u> described as: "The Dominion's most important speedboat regatta since the secession last year of Region #13 of the A.P.B.A. to form the new Canadian Boating Federation.(30) The course over St. Francis Bay, located between Lake Ontario and Lake St. Louis on the St. Lawrence River was 2 ½ miles in length, and before a crowd of 50,000, Bill Braden won the 225 Class Division I event with an average speed of 74.013 m.p.h. piloting his **Ariel IV** to victory.(31) <u>Boating Magazine</u> had this assessment of the weekend:

> The Valleyfield Regatta of 1951 was of the same high caliber of past years. Although hampered by a postponement for weather, a rearranged program was improvised and carried out successfully to completion. In the three heat 225 class division one event, Bill Braden of Hamilton gave away two places in the first heat to come back with wins in the second and third heats with a nerve tingling performance that had the large crowd leaning precariously over the harbor seawall to catch every weave and bounce of the '**Ariel IV**' as she zoomed ahead of her rivals. Jack Langmuir's '**Running Wild II**' had an off day; failing to finish in two of the three heats and not starting in the other. Another disappointment was '**Canada Boy**' driven by Bernard Daoust…. (32)

Braden's third and two firsts gave him the victory over fellow Hamiltonian Art Hatch, whose **Costa Lotta** had a fourth and two seconds. Bernard Daoust had a first, a D.N.F., and a 5th place. Bob Bogie had a 2nd and a .D.N.F. for his day's efforts.

On the following weekend, the Hamilton Power Boat Association staged its 3rd annual Regatta. Prior to the race, Braden was written up in the <u>Hamilton News</u>:

> A group of Hamilton newsmen gathered at Thompson's docks on the Bay Friday night to watch Bill Braden give the gun to his racing boat **Ariel IV.** …It was the first trial in several weeks, the boat having been slightly damaged at a racing meet some weeks ago….Braden looked like a man from Mars---deep-set crash helmet on head, life jacket with heavy padding around the neck, large goggles set over the eyes, and carrying a gun like contraption with which he squirted fluid into the three carburetors to bring the motor to life….after a few attempts it sprang to life with a mighty roar, and he was off in a cloud of spray….after a short warm-up, Braden began an exhibition of speed driving which fairly took the breath away…driving at speeds varying from 50 to 90 miles an hour, the fishtail of water following the boat rose to a height of 25 feet or more as Braden cut loose…the boat runs on pure alcohol-no wonder it goes crazy….(33)

More than 5000 fans were in attendance, lining the shore and the roads overlooking the course:

> Spills were few…but thrills were a dime a dozen on Hamilton Bay on Saturday afternoon ….and the majority left quite satisfied that the outstanding feature was the hydroplane inboard event captured by Bill Braden of Waterdown in straight heats. Speeds up to 90 m.p.h. were reached by the winning craft, which came from behind on both occasions to nail the early leaders.
>
> Six boats went to the starting line with Bill Braden at the wheel of **Ariel IV**, Bob Schroeder of Buffalo with **My Ambition**, Don MacDonald of Hamilton with **Mac IV**, W. Hall (Burlington) with **Royal Muskoka**, Charley Irish (Hamilton) with **Cheetah**, Charley Arnold (Hamilton) with **See Me Go**, and Bill Hodgson (Toronto) with **My Ruthie**.
>
> Hodgson went to the post against the advice of his physician. The Toronto driver suffered a severe attack of the 'flu' during the week and was instructed to stay in bed, but the excitement forced him to disregard his doctor, and he made the trip here to compete in the big event.
>
> For a time it looked…if Hodgson would be crowned winner. In the first heat, he was away flying while Braden found his motor a little cool, and the race was well advanced before the Waterdown skipper began getting the right results. Once he hit top speed, Braden ran over the field and caught the leaders some fifty yards from the finish line. Hodgson finished second and Bob Schroeder was third. (34)

In the Regatta at Gravenhurst, the Waterdown boat won her class, posting heat finishes of 1st and 2nd, to defeat American Rae Gassner who attained a second and a third. <u>Boating Magazine</u> had this view of the day's races:

> Gravenhurst Rotary Club's regatta always serves up thrill upon thrill as the public get a close view of the lower turn which is only a few hundred yards from the finish line…. Langmuir and Braden put on a very special tussle for the population in the second heat of the 225 Class Division I race-but as far as the result went, Braden's win in the first heat-which Langmuir failed to finish, put the race on 'ice' for him….(35)

At Picton on 6 August 1951, **Ariel** clocked a time of 100.141 m.p.h., as well as reaching a speed of 78.775 m.p.h. in a five mile competition. The <u>Picton Times</u> gave its readers the flavor of the excitement that took place on its waters that August weekend:

At long last, Canada holds the fourteen year old Prince Edward Yacht Club Gold Cup. First awarded in 1937, the Centennial year of the town of Picton, the famous international trophy will remain for at least one year at Brockville, Ontario.

Jack Langmuir of Brockville is the first Canadian to win this trophy. It was the first time in the history of the Prince Edward Yacht Club that three Canadian 225 Division I hydroplanes crossed the finish line in first, second and third positions. It was the first time the Gold Cup race was ever dominated by Canadian drivers.

As usual, there was a jinx. Every running of the Gold Cup has produced some sort of jinx for one of the drivers....This year the jinx was with W.G. (Bill) Brayden of Waterdown, Ontario, a true sport if there ever was one. He took his hard luck with a smile, the juggling of five seconds of time.

Langmuir won the first five mile heat. Brayden was a close second. Brayden was first in the final heat with Langmuir second.

To declare the winners of the event, Robert Finlayson, referee, computed the elapsed times of the two boats. Brayden was declared winner by five seconds. Later, at the clubhouse, Langmuir was declared official winner. The times had been rechecked. It was found Langmuir's time figures had been credited to Brayden. When Langmuir was awarded the trophy, he said: "I am sorry it happened the way it did because Bill Brayden really trimmed me in the final heat."

Brayden came up to receive the 'Pop' Cooper Sportsmanship Trophy. When George T. Fulford of Brockville handed him the cup, Brayden declared Langmuir the official winner, and 'rightly so' he said.

Although he didn't win the Gold Cup, Bill Brayden took the T. Eaton Trophy for the fastest mile. He established a new Canadian mile record for the 225 Div. I boats at dawn Monday, driving his **Ariel IV** over the mile course at 100.141 m.p.h. The former mark was 81 m.p.h. After making a one way trip down the mile at 100.550 m.p.h., Bill Brayden had a near accident on his second run. His boat hit a swell from a small outboard. The fast moving hydroplane completely left the water leaping five feet into the air. He withdrew from the course, and made a new start, and averaged 101.141 m.p.h. on their two way run. (36)

In their regatta notes, the paper commented: "Bill Brayden was awarded the 'Pops' Cooper memorial trophy for sportsmanship. He deserved it…." (37) Bob Finlayson of the Canadian Boating Federation was effusive in his praise of the Canadian drivers during the racing season:

> Flashing over the Picton mile course on August 6 at a record breaking 100.141 mph speed earned for Bill Braden of Hamilton the right to membership in the very exclusive 100 mile-an-hour club. Driving 'Ariel IV' at wide open throttle, Braden's great performance is symbolic of the outstanding driving efforts shown by Canadian motor boat jockeys this season. At regatta after regatta in race after race, the challenge of the invading forces from the United States has been swept aside as the C.B.F.'s drivers have shown convincingly they can meet-and beat-international competition. Braden in winning his heat broke Canadian competition mark for his class with a speed of 78.775 mph. (38)

This made him the first Canadian to break the 100 m.p.h. mark, and the second on the continent to do so, after Paul Sawyer. This was trumpeted in a full page advertisement by the British American Oil Company, whose gasoline and motor oil (marine lubricants) were used in the Canadian boat as it met with these successes.(39) Other advertisers were quick to climb on the success of Bill Braden and the other successful Canadian drivers of the year. The Bulova Watch Company trumpeted itself as the 'official timepiece of the Canadian Boating Federation', and along with showing photos of **Ariel IV**, **Running Wild** and **Canada Maid II**, as well as showing the layout of the course in Picton Bay, their ad contained copy which noted:

> ….split second timing by Bulova. 1/10th of a second to racing boat drivers can seem a lifetime. 1/10th of a second can mean victory or defeat; fame or failure. To measure correctly this important flash of time, Bulova watches are used exclusively by the Canadian Boating Federation at all Motor Boat Sanctioned Regattas in Canada….The Bulova Watch Company Ltd. timing device used at all Canadian sanctioned regattas timed ten boats individually to a fraction of a second. The accuracy of these Bulova timepieces makes it possible to clock accurately world and Canadian record boat speeds over the mile and in competition. (40)

The start of September saw the Detroit Memorial, where Braden finished third in each of the two heats. Ironically he was leading in the second heat, but spun out on the last corner. As with the race at Windsor, the day ended with the Canadian boat in a third place position. Several days later, the boat was on the same course for the Silver Cup Regatta. In the first six mile heat, **Ariel IV** did not finish because her fuel line broke. She won the second heat, posting an Ederburn record for the fastest heat of 74.964 m.p.h. The combination of the results of the two heats gave her another third place finish for the weekend's work.

On Wednesday 5 September, the Canadian Regional Championships were held in the waters of Lake Ontario, just off the Canadian National Exhibition. This was a sanctioned event held under the auspices of the Canadian Boating Federation. The course was of two laps, each of 2 ½ miles duration, inside the breakwater. The launching slip was at Taylor's Boathouse, at the foot of Bathurst Street, and a crane was provided for the boat launching at no cost to any of the racers. Similarly gasoline racing fuel and oil was provided without charge by the British American Oil Company. There was no entry fee charged to any of the competitors as well. Cash prizes were offered based on finishes of first ($50), second ($30), third ($20), fourth ($10), and fifth ($5). Trophies included the Canadian National Exhibition Trophy to the driver who attained the highest number of race points in '225 Class', Division 1. In addition, the British American Oil Company Limited Trophy would go to the '225 Class', Division 1 driver who attained the highest number of race points in the class, during the year on the Canadian racing circuit.(41) Bill Braden was announced as the winner of the two trophies since he placed first in all three heats. He was the first Canadian **ever** to capture the trophy. (42) He was also the first Canadian to exceed 100 m.p.h. in such a tiny inboard craft. As well, he took home prizes of $50 in each of the heats that he won on the Toronto waterfront.

1952 Boat Racing Season

The **Ariel** boats did not race with the same frequency in the 1952 season since Bill Braden was working with the **Miss Supertest** racing team. However, **Ariel IV** was out on Gull Lake at the Gravenhurst Power Regatta, making the front page of the Globe and Mail, for all the wrong reasons. The boat was half submerged in shallow waters, and was being pushed ashore by Bill Braden. The article went on to note that "the craft was wrecked …when Braden cut too sharply on the south turn, ripping out the port sponson".(43) Jack Langmuir, driving **Running Wild II** ended up capturing the Labatt Trophy before a crowd of 4200 spectators. It had been a close race through the first heat when Braden ended up second to Langmuir. The Hamilton Spectator was slightly more graphic in its description of what transpired: "…took her around one turn too sharply and ripped off a sponson. The sleek craft partially submerged, and had to be towed to shore where it sank in shallow water."(44)

1953 Boat Racing Season

In 1953, Bill Braden was back racing his own boat. At the Detroit Memorial on 4 July, held some five weeks before the Gold Cup race at Seattle, Washington, **Ariel IV** ended up second overall, after a second place in the first heat, while winning the second heat with a 69.971 m.p.h. speed. This regatta was the seventh annual contest sponsored by the Detroit River Racing Association, which would later come to be known as the Windmill Point Yacht Club. Police estimated that there were some 75,000 boating fans in attendance along the shores of the Detroit River. As a Detroit newspaper described the day:

> ....By all counts, it was a perfect regatta. The waters around the course were smooth. Just enough of a ripple in the light downriver breeze to avoid an oily calm ....There was no confusion in the pits, in the press box, or on the course at any time. There were all kinds of thrills on the Detroit River for the speedboat bugs.... (45)

Ariel IV in the pit area in Detroit.

At the Silver Cup, from 5-7 September, she led for the first half of a lap, but lost it as the Detroit River was very rough, to come in fourth place . Combined with a first place finish in the second heat, her totals for the day led to a second place standing. She ran the fastest heat of the day with an attained speed of 67.9 m.p.h.

Ariel IV being swung out into the Detroit River.

Bill Braden in the cockpit of Ariel IV prior to leaving the pit area.

Young Billy Braden watching events in the pit area in Detroit. In the background in the cockpit of Ariel IV is Gil Zamprogna, who worked with Bill Braden at the Hamilton Street Railway, and went on to become his lead mechanic with both Ariel and Miss Supertest.

Bill Braden, and his brother, John accompany their Dad to the 1953 Detroit Memorial Regatta, where Ariel IV finished in second place.

Bill Braden approaches the shoreline in Ariel IV, and prepares to throw a towline to the shore

At the end of the summer, Toronto staged its first full scale international speedboat regatta on the C.N.E. waterfront. Though Bill Braden's name was not mentioned in the results of the race, some quotes from the article give the flavor of what it was like to race in Lake Ontario in the postwar years:

> This regatta…should provide the most spectacular races and the most dangerous of any on the circuit because they'll be held inside the breakwater. It's going to be dynamic….The long straightaways to get up high speed and then those short turns. The danger will be imminent…particularly for those fast babies, the 266 cu in boats which whiz along at the fastest clip.

> ….The thrill of speedboat racing seems to be the prime attraction for the drivers because the pay is practically miniscule. The winner of a heat gets $30…and the most a driver could make would be about $720-$800, and a lot of them never make a dime. So it's the thrills, the glory and the beautiful trophies that are up for competition.

> The circuit in Ontario embraces Arnprior, Gananoque, Gravenhurst, Brockville, Picton and Toronto. It also stretches into Quebec ,and continues after Toronto to Buffalo.(46)

1954 Boat Racing Season

On the holiday weekend in early July 1954, Braden entered **Ariel IV** in the International Nickel Cup Regatta, sponsored by the Gananoque Chamber of Commerce. Before a crowd of 4,000 spectators on the river bank, Braden and defending champion Bernard Daoust of Lachine, Quebec in **Canada Maid** were both disqualified from the first heat for crossing the starting line ahead of the gun. Daoust went on to win the final heat and end up second to **Escapade I** of Montreal, the ultimate winner; while Braden posted a second place in the second heat to end the regatta in fourth place overall.(47)

While racing **Miss Supertest II**, in Detroit, Bill Braden also found the time to put **Ariel IV** through her racing paces at the Detroit Memorial. She placed a third, after winning the opening heat with a speed of 73.0 m.p.h., followed by a heat where she did not finish. He also raced her in the 135 class, pulling in two third place finishes to obtain a third place. Later in the summer, he entered the Silver Cup Regatta where he came in sixth or seventh place. He wrote in his notes that Harry Greening was in attendance at that race. (48)

1955 & 1956 Boat Racing Seasons

In both these years, Bill Braden was so involved in driving **Miss Supertest** that he did not enter his **Ariel** boats in any racing competitions.

Chapter 6 –The **Miss Supertest** Years

Prior to the Canadian challenge in 1950 for the Harmsworth Trophy, Harold Wilson of Ingersoll, Ontario, owner of **Miss Canada III** and **Miss Canada IV**, Canada's top unlimited class racing boats announced his retirement from the field of unlimited racing. Early in 1951, both boats were put on sale.

Jim Thompson, son of the owner of the Supertest Petroleum Company of London, Ontario, wrote:

> ….since these were Canadian boats, we felt they should remain in Canada, and in all probability if they left the country, it could mean the end of unlimited class boat racing insofar as Canada is concerned.(1)

Negotiating through Mr. F.J. Moore of Reliance Petroleum, one of Supertest's subsidiaries, they offered $5500 for the two hulls and the two engines, which was accepted by the Wilsons, thus ensuring that the boats did not end up in the United States.

For the next month after the purchase, the Thompsons consulted with a number of boating experts both in Canada and the United States, about how to prepare the boat for racing competitions. One of these experts, John Hacker, a Detroit based naval architect, recommended that the Thompsons obtain the driving services of Bill Braden. Hacker referred to Braden as "the best driver in Canada", and one who "could get everything that is in a boat out of it". (2)

It is fascinating how quickly Bill Braden's name came to the fore in the press as the possible driver of the new Canadian hydroplane. The <u>Globe and Mail</u> was the first to refer to him in that role:

> The unlimited powerboat, **Miss Canada IV**, we learned yesterday, will race in the Silver Cup event at Detroit this Labor Day weekend under the name of **Miss**

Supertest....Her driver is to be decided. It may be Bill Braden of Hamilton, or an American professional. (3)

The <u>Hamilton Spectator</u> was the next one to pick up on the scent of this story:

....the Silver Cup will be held Monday....but it is rumored that he [Braden] will drive the former **Miss Canada** now known as **Miss Supertest**....it is not known whether the boat will be ready for either of these big events {Henry Ford Memorial and Silver Cup], but Braden's name has been linked with the boat for several months. He is rated one of the finest speedboat drivers in Canada.(4)

Finally, the word came from the driver himself that all the rumors were indeed true:

If **Miss Supertest**, now undergoing changes in Sarnia, can be made ready for the President's Cup race, which will be held in Washington two weeks from today, W.G. Braden from Waterdown will be the driver. It was revealed this morning by Mr. Braden, from his summer home in Milford Bay that he had been engaged to drive the speedster, and that he expects to leave for Sarnia shortly for time trials.... Bill Braden did announce that while the boat will be lighter, and not quite so fast, he expected big things from the boat and so does Col. Gordon Thompson, London, new owner of the speedster....(5)

Mechanical difficulties and gearbox issues predominated, so that **Miss Supertest** did not race during the 1951 racing season.

In 1952, they attempted to make the boat ready for the Windsor Yacht Club's Maple Leaf Regatta. In mid-June, the boat was lowered into the St. Clair River for the first time in order to test out her Rolls Royce Merlin engine. With Bill Braden behind the wheel, and Charlie Volker in the mechanic's seat, the boat attained the speed of 110 mph in one test run, and looked like she could compete with any American boat.

But on race day, the bad luck that had previously plagued this boat, came back to haunt her. She failed to complete her qualifying run before the start of the race, and did not compete in Heat #1. Prior to the second heat, the Thompsons were told that they could run in the race and qualify, as long as they attained a speed of 65 mph during the first lap. On the first turn, **Miss Supertest** was close to **Miss Pepsi**, but the American boat moved into the lead in the backstretch. Entering the lower turn, the Canadian boat's gearbox burned out, and she did not come out of the turn, floating to a stop. **Miss Supertest's** afternoon had lasted less than one lap around the course, and Colonel Gordon Thompson penned the following words to Bill Braden:

Just a line to say many thanks for being with us at Windsor on Saturday, and to congratulate you on the most excellent start.

It was disappointing that conditions did not permit the boat to continue. However, we must benefit from our experiences and I well recall my expression of a year ago that we would not attempt to race until everything was in 'apple-pie' order and tests carried out under conditions at least as severe as those to be expected in racing....Looking beyond, and assuming that we get the kinks out of her, I foresee the possibility of working up to a Harmsworth challenge through either duplicating the present boat (when she is right) at one-half her weight and using the Merlin engine, or perhaps bringing the Griffon engines back here, which I am confident we can do through our English connections.

I have never doubted that we must work up to the peak gradually and am looking forward to obtaining some worthwhile data and good results before this season is out. (6)

The only positive point to come out of the 1952 unlimited boat racing season was the realization that there was a strong fan base for the Canadian boat:

....while our entry...was not successful in winning due to the development of mechanical trouble, I do feel that we received a tremendous amount of publicity. The boat, even while being transported on the trailer, created a tremendous interest, and even the procedure of unloading her with the crane into the water, drew a large crowd of newspaper reporters and photographers, as well as a great many amateur photographers. During the running of the second heat when **Miss Supertest** came up to the starting line neck and neck with **Miss Pepsi**, it was very evident that the Canadian boat was the popular favorite. When **Miss Supertest** was eliminated... the expressions of opinion were nothing but sympathetic... (7)

The damage to the boat was such that the only other race they could enter her into in that racing season was the Labor Day running of the Silver Cup on the Detroit River. Bill Braden qualified for the race with a lap speed of 64.240 mph on the first lap, and 53.053 mph on the second lap before mechanical problems again ended her day early. The Thompsons were both disappointed, but optimistic for the future:

....Even with hard luck, there seems to be evidence that with mechanical stability and some slight change in the wheel (propeller), we might be fully competitive with the other boats that were in the race....

I cannot tell you how sorry I feel that circumstances had to be as they were with the gearbox, but **Miss Supertest's** turn will come....(8)

During the winter of 1952-1953, Colonel Gordon Thompson managed to bid successfully on and purchase four Rolls-Royce Griffon Mark VI's: engines that had powered Seafire aircraft during World War II. They were surplus to the needs of the Canadian Armed Forces, and were sold by the Crown Assets Disposal Corporation, at a fraction of the price at which they were built. The engines reached the London Supertest plant at the end of March 1953.

Now the Thompsons had the engines they wanted for 1953. The other problem that had plagued them for two years was the gearbox. They decided to replace the previous spur type gearbox with a planetary gearbox, similar to the design previously used by the Wilsons with the boats. It was built by Bruce Wells from Wells Foundry in London, Ontario. The plan for the year was to prepare **Miss Supertest** for one day of competition: on Labor Day in the five heat, sixty mile running of the Silver Cup. The summer was spent installing the new supercharged Rolls Royce Griffon VI engine, which was capable of developing 2500 rpm, and turning the propeller through the gearbox at the rate of 7200 rpm.(9)

On her first trial on 1 September 1953, **Miss Supertest** attained the speed of 85 mph, which was about 55 mph less than they thought she would go. On 4 September, in the St. Clair River, with Jim Thompson behind the wheel, her speed was raised to a more acceptable 125 mph. On the Friday, the boat was moved to Detroit, but arrived too late to take a qualifying test. In the interim, the mechanics installed a new starter, as well as a water scoop for cooling the Griffon engine. Her performance improved enough that on the afternoon of Labor Day, Bill Braden qualified for the race at a speed of 76.163 mph. The boat seemed ready to go.

On race day, there were different expectations in the pit area. The Thompsons hoped that she might finish a race for the first time. No one expected that she might challenge for victory. The eyes of all the fans were focused on **Slo-Mo-Shun V** from Seattle, which was the prohibitive favorite. What transpired? In Heat #1, Braden with Vic Leghorn driving with him as mechanic, ended a distant sixth of the boats that did finish, only beating two boats that had dropped out with engine difficulties. In the last lap of the second heat, she came down with engine problems, and did not finish the race. As the only V-bottomed hydroplane in the race, she had a tendency to rock back and forth on the turns, where she was surpassed by the Seattle and Detroit three pointers. Jim Thompson, though disappointed in the result, was keen to persevere in their racing efforts: "....I am certainly looking forward to different conditions in the future assuming that we are to continue in the sport, which I think we should, for surely Canada should have at least one Unlimited class boat."(10)

Throughout the autumn, testing continued on the boat and the Thompsons came to realize that they needed to get a boat with a more up to date design, if they were to successfully compete for the Harmsworth Trophy. Colonel Gordon Thompson wrote to Harry Greening:

> We had purchased the boat from Wilson, and had something to get started with and with which to gain experience, and I have no regrets…excepting that we did not discover how flexible the hull was-that is to say, how badly it twisted-before we had broken two gear boxes, which made things look rather badly, in the eyes of the fans…. We fully realize that any thought of issuing such a challenge [for the Harmsworth Trophy] involves working out a boat, which we consider fully capable.(11)

In looking at getting a modern three pointer, the Thompsons met with boat builder Les Staudacher from Kawkawlin, Michigan, who promised to construct them a boat within six weeks at the cost of $5800. Construction took place at the MacCraft plant in Sarnia, Ontario, so that the boat could be entered in a Harmsworth challenge in the future. (12) The boat was thirty-one feet long, with a beam of twelve feet. It was to be constructed out of mahogany, the bow of a fir-plywood combination, while the stern was mahogany and plywood. The frame would be made of oak and spruce. The engine was to be a 7500 pound Rolls Royce Griffon. She was granted the racing number "CA 1" by the Canadian Boating Federation.

Prior to Labor Day, **Miss Supertest II** was brought to Detroit, to compete against thirteen American boats in the largest field to date, for the Silver Cup. Two days before the race, she attempted to qualify at the minimum qualifying speed of 85 mph. She could only reach the speed of 82.073 mph, and at the same time, burned out a piston. The Thompsons wanted to compete in the race to gauge their boat against the American competition. They called Wells Foundry in London and asked them to remove a cylinder bank from one of the other Griffon engines on site. Jim Thompson drove back to London at 1 am to pick up the parts, and they were back in Detroit by 9 am. After six hours of labor in 99 degree heat, the boat was ready to be put back in the Detroit River. On her final attempt to qualify on Monday morning, she burned out a second piston and was unable to qualify. Jim Thompson's views of what happened were more long range:

> ….It is, of course, regrettable, that the boat was unable to race but we are not downhearted, for…our interest is not the mere winning of one of these races, but rather that we may develop a strong contender, thus leading to the issuance of a challenge for the Harmsworth Trophy in the hope of bringing home this coveted honor.(13)

His father was more succinct in his observations: "….the year commenced with high hopes and ended on Labor Day in ignominious failure…." (14)

Over the winter of 1954-1955, the British Air Ministry agreed to release to the Thompsons two Rolls Royce Griffon 57 engines for the new boat, marking the first time that such an engine had been used in a racing boat. As well, changes were made to the carburetors of the Griffon V engines. This change would ensure that the boat could reach the speed to attain a Canadian speed record, which was to be attempted this racing season as well. The plan for the year was to get the London boat entered into as many races as possible, to provide driving experience in her for Bill Braden. At the start of May 1955, the boat was taken out of winter storage, and she was put in the waters of the St. Clair River for initial testing, with Bill Braden at the wheel. In June, they installed the new Rolls Royce 57 in the boat, and entered her into Windsor's Maple Leaf Regatta. The Hamilton Spectator was quick to address the local link in the Supertest story:

> William G. 'Bill' Braden, noted Hamilton speedboat owner and driver, will pilot Canada's only unlimited craft, **Miss Supertest II** in the Maple Leaf International Cup race at Windsor on June 18 and in the Memorial Cup race at Detroit on June 25, it was announced at London yesterday, by James G. Thompson.

> …The Hamilton sportsman who has competed all over the continent in speedboat classics, is rated Canada's top driver and has attained many honors in his own craft, notably the **Ariel IV**, and drove **Miss Canada** on several occasions.(15)

Seven American boats qualified for the race, including Joe Schoenith's **Gale IV** and **Gale V**, the latter being the defending champion in the Regatta. The course was three miles in length, and five circuits of the course would give the required fifteen miles for a heat. The goal of the Thompsons was a simple one: that their new boat would be able to see its way through to the end of a race: a feat her predecessor had been unable to accomplish.

Racing conditions were perfect that day, with just enough of a breeze to ripple the water's surface. In the morning, **Miss Supertest II** qualified at a speed of 81.203 mph, far beyond the qualifying speed of 98.25 mph attained by the Detroit boat **Such Crust III**. At the start of Heat #1, her engine refused to start, but just before the starting gun, Bill Braden was able to coax it into life, though he was last of the eight boats to cross the starting line. Then he moved up on the outside, and was able to pass all boats, save **Miss Cadillac**, for a second place finish, some twenty seconds behind the leader. Her average speed for the heat was 90.762 mph, and this was accomplished despite the engine cowling blowing off.

Bill Braden passes Chuck Thompson's Short Circuit in the first heat of the 1955 Maple Leaf Regatta.

In Heat #2, it appeared that Braden had been outmaneuvered by the Americans at the one minute gun, and that he would be stuck far back in the pack. But he noticed that two boats crossed the starting line early and were disqualified, and the others were forced to throttle back to avoid the same fate. He timed his run perfectly, hitting the line at full bore, smashing through the wall of water raised by the roostertails, and moved into an early lead. In passing **Gale IV** on the second turn, he got swamped by her roostertail, and stopped dead three quarters of the way around the lap. Braden would later observe: "She just stopped dead, as if the ignition had been cut off. I really don't know what happened to her. She just went dead."(16) After some ten minutes, Braden managed to get the engine to turn over again, but was now two laps behind the leader, and would finish last in sixth place.

Miss Supertest II trails Miss Cadillac and Gale V in front of the
Windsor Yacht Club at the 1955 Maple Leaf Regatta.

But it would be in the final heat that Bill Braden showed his driving expertise. He moved **Miss Supertest II** to the front shortly after the start. On three different occasions, on laps two, four and five, he was challenged for the lead by Lee Schoenith in **Gale V**. In the final heat, the American boat moved into the lead, but on the final straightaway, Braden regained the lead to win the heat by a mere ten feet. **Gale IV** ended up third, only one and a half seconds behind her sister. Braden averaged 99.457 mph in the final heat, and 109 mph on one lap, setting two Regatta records for fastest lap and heat. The day was a noteworthy success for Canadian unlimited hydroplane racing, for it marked the first time ever that a Canadian boat had ever finished a heat at Windsor, as well as the first time they had ever won a heat there. It also marked the first time that a Canadian unlimited had won a heat since the 1946 President's Cup race. Final standings gave the win to **Miss Cadillac**, at 869 points, while the London boat came in second with 795 points surpassing six other American entrants, including the two **Gale** boats.

Bill Braden gives a wave as the drives into the pit area at Windsor in 1955.
He brought his boat in for a second place finish on the day

The London Free Press was eloquent in its praise:

> When **Miss Supertest** won the third and final heat of the Maple Leaf International unlimited speedboat classic at Riverside early Saturday evening, it sounded like Times Square on New Year's Eve. The hundreds of boats anchored just outside the regatta course…let loose with their whistles and horns in a cacophony of sound that mingled with the cheers of the thousands who lined the Canadian side of the Detroit River.

> Even veteran sportswriters and photographers, those representing Canadian newspapers of course, who usually hide their feelings behind sphinx-like poker faces joined in the general jubilation which caused no end of chaos and confusion in a crowded press section. Most of them had been enduring the jibes and snide remarks from U.S. writers and cameramen for years because of the dismal

showings made by Canuck entries….And the Canadians made the most of **Miss Supertest**'s victory.

Miss Supertest's owners, J. Gordon Thompson and his son Jim, of London… couldn't hide their joy either. And they weren't to be blamed! The Thompsons, usually extremely staid and reserved, didn't have too much to say, but their smiles spoke volumes…as they accepted congratulatory handshakes from friends and strangers alike at the boat 'pits'.

….Bill Braden of Hamilton…took over in the Maple Leaf and the performance **Miss Supertest** gave really had the Yanks eyes a poppin. In fact, when Braden accelerated **Miss Supertest** coming around the turns, he had everybody's eyeballs revolving! (17)

Colonel Gordon Thompson was ecstatic about the boat's performance, and wrote Harry Greening to tell him about it:

Just a line to let you know that we were very pleased with the performance of the boat on Saturday, but even more in the way in which Will handled her. In all my observations on the Detroit River, I have never seen finer or more experienced driving than we saw on Saturday by Will. Jim and I feel that he deserves all the credit.

As to the boat herself, while one doesn't become excited in a single victory, nevertheless, based on the characteristics she showed, and her ability to overtake the best of them on the straightaway, the Detroit owners have every reason to be worried as we hear they are.

There is no doubt at all that had the engine not cut out in the second lap, and even with a fourth place, we would have won the trophy. However, the engine had only been in the boat a short time, and Jim had only been able to give her two test runs, and those were not under racing conditions. (18)

The success that had come to **Miss Supertest** prompted her owners to enter her in the Detroit Memorial Regatta on the following weekend. The Canadian boat immediately became the favorite in the race, based on the Maple Leaf results, as well as the fact that the Griffon 57 engine had some two hundred extra horsepower than the American Allison engines. There were nine American boats competing in the race. The ten boats crossed the starting line in a pack, with **Miss Supertest** in seventh place and moving up. On the first turn near the Belle Isle Bridge, Horace Dodge's **My Sweetie**, a old style v-bottom boat, got caught in the wakes of the leading boats, and leapt out of the water. Driver Jon Ban was pitched out of the cockpit, and into the Detroit River. The pilotless boat moved on to strike Danny Foster's **Tempo VII** on her right hand side. Just like an errant pinball, the Dodge-owned boat careened back into the middle of the course. She now sped towards Bud Saile's **Miss Cadillac,** which swerved to avoid her, and ended up striking **Miss Supertest**. The crash tore off the left sponson ,and ripped a hole in her left side. Bill Braden did not cast any blame on Bud Saile: "I saw **Miss Cadillac** coming at me from my left, and tried to pull away, but she bounced right against me. I'm not blaming Frank Saile. He probably was forced to do it, to get away from the boat that was running all over the course". (19)

He also added:

> There was little danger of sinking, but things were hectic for a few minutes, and of course, we were definitely out of the race. I believe the boat, as it started on Saturday, would have passed all tests successfully. Now we've got to repair the craft, tinker with a few gadgets; try it out on the St. Clair River about July 13, in a competition there. If it comes up to expectations, then we'll probably challenge for races at Seattle and the Gold Cup. (20)

Those in attendance at the race were surprised by the sudden bad luck that befell the Canadian boat:

> The Detroit policeman…at the speedboat racing pits…gazed at the gaping hole in **Miss Supertest**'s hull. It was a sympathetic gaze, which seemed to say: 'You have the darndest luck'. He turned to this writer with a wry smile: 'Y'know', he said. 'I was so sure that she was going to win the race today that I took two to one odds on her.

> The gendarme wasn't the only one disappointed at **Miss Supertest**'s ill luck. There were hundreds of speedboat racing fans, both Canadians and Americans, who eagerly anticipated a winning performance from the London entry…in the Ford Memorial Trophy race. The Yanks, like us, are great ones to root for the underdog…and Canadian speedboats have been underdogs in unlimited events for so long…many of Uncle Sam's citizens were hoping that **Miss Supertest**, after her spectacular showing in the Maple Leaf a week ago…would win this one.

> The Thompsons, J. Gordon, and his son, Jim, were among those obviously chagrined over what happened. Even if they didn't say so in so many words…we felt they thought that their sleek craft would emerge as the top boat in Saturday's classic.

If the Thompsons, pere et fils, had thrown up their hands…and said 'that's it', or 'enough's enough', no one could honestly blame them. Perhaps those with less interest, and enthusiasm in bringing a Harmsworth Trophy to Canada, or even a world's record…would have done exactly that. They've been in speedboat racing long enough about these setbacks….As Jim Thompson put it: 'That's racing for you'. (21)

Prognosis for the boat's recovery improved upon her return to Sarnia. One large hole was discovered at the front of the left sponson, with a smaller one further back. Fortunately the hull was not breached, and it was felt that with the necessary repairs, she would be ready in time for the St. Clair race on 17 July.

A crowd of 65,000 gathered on both sides of the international border to watch this race. The course was laid out at 2 ½ miles, with one mile straightaways, and one quarter mile turns. The race would be three heats of 15 miles each, totaling 45 miles duration. Ten American boats and **Miss Supertest** showed up. Only six boats qualified for the race, and the number was reduced to five boats when **Dora My Sweetie**, out for an early afternoon test run, hit something in the water, and sank at the pits. In the opening heat, by the end of Lap #1, Braden trailed **Such Crust** by three to four boat lengths. In the second lap, an area of front decking on the boat came loose, which forced Bill Braden to slow down. It turned out that the boat was not balanced correctly to deal with the choppy water conditions. Her average speed for the heat was a slow 66.182 m.p.h. Race officials gave an extra fifteen minutes prior to the second heat for repairs to be effected on the Canadian boat. In Heat #2, she crossed the starting line behind **Such Crust**, and then had a duel with **Miss Cadillac** for the runner up position. By the end of the heat, **Miss Supertest** got second place, with the higher average speed of 71.689 m.p.h. Prior to the final heat; the mechanics changed both her propeller and her battery. In the final heat, she had an early lead, but lost it by the end of the first lap. In the first turn of lap #2, her engine quit, and would not restart. The Canadian boat ended up in third place on the day with 525 points, based on her 3rd, 2nd, and D.N.F., trailing **Such Crust** and **Miss Cadillac**, but ahead of **Wha Hoppen Too** and **Short Circuit**. Gordon Thompson wrote a memo about what had happened on the weekend:

"On the subject of power, on two occasions (one of those yesterday), I have chatted with Will [Braden] about unlimited power over 2200 r.p.m., and the fact that Les [Staudacher], in driving the boat, referred to it as 'a bomb', and of [Ted] Jones saying the power 'scared' him.

Will has said to me twice that he doesn't understand this, and that nothing he has done with the boat, either at Sarnia, or at Windsor, or in the lake, gave him any such impression from the angle of a race driver. Maybe we haven't any more power at the upper end than we need. (22)

Rolls Royce studied the damaged engine, and noted that the engine was operating at 2500 r.p.m., with the supercharger turning the propeller at a rate of 11,000 r.p.m. When the boat became airborne because of the rough water, the propeller would leave the water, and without having to worry about the resistance of the water, both engine and propeller would rev up by several hundred extra r.p.m.'s. When the boat landed back in the water, and the propeller went back under the surface, the engine was slowed back to 2500 r.p.m. in the fraction of a second, thus putting a real strain on the supercharger drive.

Three and a half weeks later, the boat came out of the MacCraft shop, and was placed on the St. Clair River once again. They key in the future was to keep the boat in the water, and running efficiently on all three points. During the time that the boat was being repaired, the Thompson family were joined by Bill Braden and mechanic Bruce Wells in attending the Gold Cup races in Seattle, with the hope of learning from the other race boat teams that were on site. Ironically Bill Braden drove **Miss Cadillac** in the 1955 Gold Cup race on behalf of owner, Frank Saile Jr. The boat had qualified at a speed of 96.222 m.p.h. In the first heat, the owner had driven her to a fifth place finish. Braden was behind the wheel in both the second and third heats, where he posted finishes of fifth place and fourth place.(23) Under both men, **Miss Cadillac** did not play a key role in any part of this 48th annual running of the Gold Cup in Seattle, Washington. What it did was to allow the Thompsons and Bill Braden to see how an American racing team prepared for and operated in one of the biggest races on the A.P.B.A. racing calendar, and to gauge how this boat matched up as a potential competitor.

On their return in mid-August, different acceleration tests were done at Sarnia, trying out different gear ratios and propeller combinations. The boat was then brought to Detroit for the Silver Cup race. Eleven Detroit based boats, one from Seattle, and **Miss Supertest II** were the contestants. Two and a half hours before their heat, the Canadians found a problem with the gearbox, and the mechanics tore it apart, but could not put it back together in time for their entry in the heat. She was allowed to take the position of another boat in the second round of elimination heats. So running in Heat 2B, she was dueling for second place with **Miss Detroit**, one half mile behind **Miss Thriftway**. Ultimately she would end up in third place, and Bill Braden reported that on all three laps at the same position (the short buoy on the upper turn), he heard a popping noise in his engine, and each time he would see a flash or spark on the top of the engine. That one heat was her sum total racing for the day, as she did not have enough points to move on to Heat #3. Danny Foster, driving Guy Lombardo's boat **Tempo VII**, would win the race, marking Lombardo's first triumph on the Detroit River, since his victory in the 1947 Gold Cup.

What bothered the Thompsons the most was that the Griffon engine was only able to put out a maximum 2900 r.p.m.'s. The engine would not rev up beyond that point and Bill Braden ran out of power. It marked the first time in using the Griffon that power was unavailable at the top end, but nothing untoward was found during the post race examination of the exterior of the engine. There would be further discussions about gear ratios and propeller pitch.

After Jim Thompson took the boat out and set a new speed record of 112.5 m.p.h. on a measured mile at the Canadian National Exhibition, the fastest speed ever attained by a hydroplane on the waterfront, the boat was shipped back to Sarnia, where the gear ratio was changed prior to a return to competitive racing. Thompson had been able to get 3100 r.p.m. out of her in Toronto, and it was hoped that there would be no further problems. Bill Braden took the boat out on the St.Clair River on 8 September, and after a couple of laps, started hearing a popping noise while the boat was turning. During an investigation on shore, a crack was discovered in the supercharger front casing. This problem forced the Thompsons to withdraw from competing in the President's Cup, and was a disappointing end to the 1955 racing season.

But once a new supercharger had been ordered and the engine rebuilt, the plan was to prepare the boat to attempt both a Canadian and world speed record on the waters at the Long Reach in Picton in early November. The first attempt was to eclipse the Canadian speed record. The gear ratio was altered, with subsequent days of testing in the St. Clair River. In late October, the boat was moved up to Picton and tested on the local waters from the 26th through the 30th. The plan had been to make the attempt on that last day, since the Canadian Boating Federation had been given official sanction for the 30th by the Union of International Motor boating in Belgium. They waited seven hours for water conditions to improve, but ultimately the attempt had to be scrubbed due to rain with winds of up to 35 m.p.h. They hoped to go on the following day. Halloween dawned sunny, cool and clear, with a temperature of about 60 degree Fahrenheit. In the morning, there were seven trial runs before Danny Foster pronounced the boat ready for the trial.

The course was a five mile straightaway running in a north-south direction in the Long Reach, some six miles from Picton. The first two miles allowed the boat to accelerate, the middle mile was the test area and the final two miles gave a distance to decelerate. The course had to be run once in each direction, and the average speed of the two times would be the mile speed.

As Bill Braden approached the measured mile along the two mile run-in, he felt the boat roll a little, but thought that it had been caused by a passing wave. With a roostertail fifty feet high and trailing two hundred feet behind the boat. Braden entered the mile and came out with a speed of 155.844 m.p.h. Going in the opposite direction, he reached a speed of 153.846 m.p.h., which when averaged out, set a new Canadian speed record of 154.845 m.p.h., beating **Miss Canada IV**'s 1949 record of 138.58 m.p.h. The recognized world record for propeller driven craft was the

178.2 m.p.h. set by Stanley Sayrs' boat **Slo-Mo-Shun.** The recent run of 202.32 m.p.h. set by Donald Campbell, was not recognized in North America, because it was set in a jet-powered boat. The boat finished the mile test and was still running well, so Bill Braden headed off to see if he could up the Canadian record to a higher speed. He finished one lap through the mile, when the motor stopped, and the boat was towed into the Prince Edward Yacht Club. What prevented her from sinking in the Bay of Quinte was the fact that her hull was packed with styrofoam planks, mostly in the nose and the sponsons. Without the styrofoam, the boat would sit very low in the water, and would have a hard time starting because of her nose heaviness. Surprisingly, a hole some 2.5 inches in diameter was found in the crankcase. The stabilizer fin and the air trap on the port side were also gone, and the sponson was damaged as well. They came to the conclusion that the boat had run over a small log. It was amazing that she had been able to set a speed record while in such a damaged state! Bill Braden was quoted as saying: "She still had a slight bounce to her, and I certainly didn't open her right up…." (24)

The boat was returned to London for examination under Rolls-Royce supervision. The conclusion was that the propeller had been strained beyond its capacity. The boat was then returned to Sunningdale Farm for the winter.

On 28 December, the long awaited dream of Jim Thompson and his father came true. The Canadian Boating Federation issued a challenge for the Harmsworth Trophy, in the following words:

> The Canadian Boating Federation hereby challenges the Yachtsmen's Association of America to race in 1956 for the B.I.T., also known as the Harmsworth Trophy, and now held by your organization. We have selected to represent us in this contest, the Unlimited class hydroplane, Miss Supertest, owned by Messrs. [Gordon] Thompson and [Jim] Thompson of London, Ontario. We have selected as driver, Mr. William Braden of Hamilton, Ontario. (25)

This was the first challenge for the Harmsworth Trophy, since the Wilsons had made their attempt in 1950. The question was whether the Thompsons dream would become a reality in the next racing season?

On 8 May, **Miss Supertest II** was lowered into the water at the Mac Craft slip. Over the winter, the boat's tail fin had been removed. Positively it helped stabilize the boat, but it both gave trouble on the turns, and acted as a sail, pulling the boat to one side. This made the ride a lot more difficult for the driver, who had to fight to keep the boat on course. They also cut back on the fiberglass cowling to better streamline the nose, and lessen the resistance of the wind.

The first challenge for the re-designed boat was at the running of the Windsor Regatta on 23 June. This was a sanctioned race where the American boats would compete for the right to represent their country in the Harmsworth challenge. A large contingent of American boats were on hand. To qualify, boats would have to have an average speed greater than 75 m.p.h. Three fifteen mile heats were planned on the course located between the Windsor Yacht Club on one side and Peche Island on the other, in what was described as "the toughest and tightest race course in Canada and the U.S."(26)

Nine boats qualified, one of which was **Miss Supertest II**, with her speed of 77.14 m.p.h. Bill Braden described the ride in this fashion: "She was really rocking and rolling out there this morning. It was especially hard on the turns. We're going to have to keep our speeds down to keep from cracking up. Maybe the Americans will take chances, but they've got a dozen boats. We've got only one Harmsworth challenger".(27) After a heat was completed successfully, the weather turned miserable, with a 25 minute delay of Heat 1-B, while torrential showers soaked the thousands of spectators along the Riverside shoreline. The heat was run, soon followed by a 35 m.p.h. wind, and a second torrential downpour, which knocked out the electrical equipment, and turned the pits and parking lot into a quagmire. The Regatta Chairman called off the rest of the race, marking the first cancellation since its 1949 inception. Using the highest average speed over the single heat as the benchmark, Bill Braden brought his boat in for a third place finish behind the winner, **Dora My Sweetie**.

Gordon Thompson wrote a confidential memo to his son after the Windsor race:

> The performances of the boat and engine at the Maple Leaf were not satisfactory. …those of us concerned were all confident that the boat was ready to go and perform well.…The Windsor experience was valuable in that it revealed that the weight distribution …has not been obtained.…Both during the qualifying period and during the heat at Windsor, the engine apparently lacked the pep that was evident at Sarnia.…W.G.B. [Bill Braden] said he called for power at Windsor, and it wasn't there. (28)

The next race in the season was the initial running of the Prince Edward Regatta at Picton Bay. It would be the first race in Canada for the unlimited hydroplanes. No cash prizes were offered, but Picton Mayor Harvey McFarland sponsored a trophy for the winner. The race course was located north of the Bethlehem Steel property, with three heats of fifteen miles each comprising the race.

In the first heat, the London based boat was a close third behind **Miss U.S.** and **Gale IV** at the beginning. At the end of the first lap she had passed all the American boats, and ended up one mile ahead of **Miss U.S.** and 11 ½ minutes ahead of **Gale IV**. Bill Braden's average speed for the heat was 78.150 m.p.h., with the fastest lap being the first one at 83.721 m.p.h. Heat #2 was a competition between **Miss Supertest** and **Miss U.S.**, with the American boat winning by some thirty yards. The final heat featured six boats. Braden was initially third behind Jack Barlow in **Miss U.S.**, and **Gale V**, but halfway around the lap he had moved up to second place. By the first turn in lap #2, he passed Bartlow on the inside, and from then on, **Miss Supertest II** stayed in front, and finished ahead by one hundred yards. Her average speed was 93.264 m.p.h., and included a Canadian fastest lap time of 95.559 m.p.h. on lap #3. The boat's performance was aided by the addition of forty-six pounds of extra weight in the form of a tarpaulin, installed at the rear transom, in the final heat of the race. It steadied the boat and reduced the pitch that had occurred in the first two heats, which had caused Bill Braden to reduce his speed. **Miss Supertest II** obtained 1100 points for her two firsts and one second place. **Miss U.S.** with her first, second and third place got 925 points. **Miss Wayne** had two first places to total 800 points and a third place finish.

Miss Supertest II drives by the Prince Edward Yacht Club as she heads for the Long Reach in 1956.

With her wake bubbling behind her, Bill Braden takes Miss Supertest
II out into the Long Reach at Picton in 1956.

The Canadian press was happy with the win and showed it:

> It took over two years: two years of heartbreak and frustrating disappointment,
> two years of working in grease and grime, two years of trial and error and
> experimenting; and yes, two years of being laughed and scoffed at; but Jim
> Thompson of London has finally caught up with his dream of owning a real,
> honest to goodness Harmsworth Trophy challenger representing Canada.
>
> All this may sound somewhat melodramatic, and even a mite corny, but
> nevertheless, it's true. Because after two years, Thompson's **Miss Supertest II**
> has come into her own....
>
> Much of the credit for the long awaited victory has to go to Braden. He drove
> superbly in every heat, but outdid himself in the final, when **Miss U.S.** grabbed

the lead and he was forced to bring the London entry from behind in one of the neatest pieces of driving in unlimited speedboat racing history....

What makes the feat even more outstanding is the fact that conditions were far from ideal. The three mile course laid out on Picton Bay was stirred up by a stiff southwest breeze that made the going extremely rough and hazardous. Braden told the <u>Free Press</u> after the race that 'it was one of the roughest rides I've ever had....' (29)

After the race, the boat was moved to Sunningdale Farm in London for an overhaul. The repairs were not completed in time for the boat to be entered in the St. Clair Regatta. Testing centered on possible fuel types, the installation of a Holley carburetor, the relocation of the rudder, and the use of different propellers and fuel pumps. The boat was damaged eight days before the race when she was hit by the wash of a passing cabin cruiser on Lake Huron, and became airborne. When she came back to the water's surface, she had a 12" x 4" hole torn in her hull. Repairs were effected at the MacCraft slip; and while this was occurring, a dozen U.S. hydroplanes from Detroit were fighting it out for the Silver Cup on the Detroit River. When these results were tallied along with the points from earlier races during the summer, the Harmsworth Selection Committee of the Yachtsmen's Association of America decided to have a showdown amongst the top six American boats to see who could best defend the Harmsworth against the challenge posed by **Miss Supertest II**. These American boats included **Shanty I** (from Seattle), and five Detroit based unlimited: **Miss U.S. II**, **Dora My Sweetie**, **Such Crust III**, **Gale V**, **Gale VI**. Gearbox woes claimed **Such Crust**. **Dora My Sweetie** could not finish her lap, and came back to the pits with a smashed hull. Joe Schoenith pulled out his two Gales with a variety of mechanical issues. **Shanty** roared around the lap and posted the fastest lap speed ever run on the Detroit River at 117.727 m.p.h., some ten miles per hour faster than previously performed. **Miss U.S. II** came in at 105.52 m.p.h., and was designated as the substitute boat if **Shanty** was unable to meet the starter's gun at the Harmsworth race.

As can be imagined, **Miss Supertest** became the darling of the Canadian media outlets as the Harmsworth competition loomed on the horizon:

What Mount Everest was to Sir Edmund Hillary; what the four minute mile was to Roger Bannister; the Harmsworth Trophy is to 29 year old Jim Thompson of London, Ontario. Late this month, Thompson sends his **Miss Supertest II**-a $200,000 prodigy of the waves-out on the waters of the Detroit River in search of the most coveted prize in speedboat racing. It's a quest that has broken the hulls and hearts of a score of challengers. The trophy has been the exclusive property of U.S. owners for more than 40 years.

...The Canadian challenger came through with flying colors in her trial runs. At Picton, late in June, the boat set a Canadian lap record of 93.264 miles an hour in a race over the choppy waters of Picton Bay....The Picton victory was a milestone for Canadian powerboat racing. It was the first time a Canadian owned craft had ever won an unlimited class race. For the Thompsons and the **Miss Supertest** crew, it was a big moment. Before the race, like all the owners of these powerful but temperamental water speedsters, they were worried about what the craft would do under competitive conditions. The boat has now proved itself. It appeared to have the speed plus the endurance for the job. Most observers agreed this would be the most serious challenge the U.S. had faced since Englishman Kaye Don almost won it back in 1930....

Danny Foster, who drove bandleader Guy Lombardo's **Miss Tempo** to victory in many racing classics was so impressed with **Miss Supertest**, he decided to campaign with her this summer instead of with Lombardo's boats. However, he won't be at the controls in the Harmsworth race. Bill Braden of Hamilton will drive the boat since rules insist that a Canadian entry must have a Canadian driver.

...The Picton trials left little doubt **Miss Supertest** had the speed. But the owners were worried because she was so difficult to handle. So she went back to Sarnia for a face-lifting job. Last winter the tail-fin, which Thompson felt 'wasn't serving any good purpose' was removed. The engine cowling was also cut down. The result was a more streamlined boat with the missing tail-fin making it unique among craft of its class. Thompson, happy with the changes made, feels the boat has lost none of its speed, and is much easier to handle and so more suitable for racing in the narrow confines of the Harmsworth course on the Detroit River.

'We like to think we took over where Wilson left off' Thompson explained. 'We are determined, just as he was, to bring Canada the Harmsworth Trophy'. The London owners have not let money stand in their way. The redesigning and building of **Miss Supertest II** are estimated to have cost $200,000. Add to that $20,000 a year maintenance and the cost of hiring drivers and crew, and it comes to a sizeable figure.... (30)

Miss Supertest II arrived in Detroit on 22 August, for three days of pre-race preparations. Issues to be checked out included the quantity and type of fuel to be used in the race. On the second day of testing, Bill Braden struck a marker buoy, damaging the propeller as well as the decking on the port side. On the final day, there was a break in the lower half of the crankcase of the Griffon VI engine, which was replaced by the Griffon 57A....

To avoid any miss-understanding of the Harmsworth rules, the International Race Commission held a pre-race meeting of the two racing teams at the Whittier Hotel on the Detroit waterfront. Immediately, a warm friendship sprung up between Bill Braden and **Shanty** driver, Colonel Russ Schleeh. Years later, Colonel Schleeh remembered those days fondly: "Bill Braden was a very fine boat driver and an outstanding man. He was a no nonsense, conscientious sort of guy and made an excellent first and lasting impression". (31)

On the day prior to the first race, the Canadian challenger had one of those 'one in a million' accidents that had plagued them over the previous five years. An inch long section from the oil fitting dropped into the gear box, causing the gears to split. The engine was replaced with the only engine that remained available: the one that powered her to victory earlier in the summer at Picton.

At the 1956 Harmsworth challenge, Bill Braden talks with Gar Wood, while Miss Supertest owner Jim Thompson (at left) chats with Harry Greening.

The First Race

The race started at 5:30 p.m. on Saturday 24 July. At the starting line, Bill Braden was ahead of the American defender by six seconds. On the first turn, **Shanty** passed her near the Detroit Boat Club, and drenched her with her roostertail. By the end of the first lap, **Shanty**'s lead was up to seventeen seconds. Her speed of 98.784 m.p.h. was the fastest lap of the day; while **Miss Supertest** did not have her fastest lap till the seventh lap with 91.976 m.p.h. Observers felt that the Griffon engine was off key and losing revolutions. The American defender had a lead of over two miles by the race's end. Bill Braden had to be assisted out of his cockpit back in the pit area, and stated: "I never took such a beating before. My hips are so sore; I don't even want to sit down. I'm sure glad there's no race today [Sunday]". (32)

After the race, Bill Braden stated: "We couldn't stay with him in rough water. Russ drove a wonderful race. We might have done better in smooth water, but **Shanty** is a fine performing boat". After getting a congratulatory handshake, Schleeh responded with: "I'm sorry for the dousing I gave you on the turn. You know I didn't mean to". (33)

Colonel Gordon Thompson was displeased with the performance of his boat:

> I was ashamed. She is better than that. She did a lap at 106 m.p.h. at Picton on a three mile course with Bill [Braden] driving her. Surely she could be expected to do much better on this five mile course which has two 2 ½ mile straightaways. We wouldn't have brought her down if we didn't think she would be better than she was. (34)

Bill Braden offered this assessment:

> There's a lot of work to be done and it has to be done in a hurry. We undoubtedly will have to change the propeller, and make some major changes in the boat's balance. She didn't ride well in the rough water. We'll probably have comparable conditions Monday, and so we have to get ready for them. The boat rode out of the water too much in the opening race, and that was the reason I had trouble staying on the throttle. (35)

Russ Schleeh offered his professional assessment from the opposite cockpit: "I think that the changing of the engines in **Miss Supertest** must have affected her balance. The way she was running Saturday, I wouldn't want to drive her. A boat out of balance is a tough thing to handle". (36)

With a day off from racing on Sunday, Canadian mechanics had a forty-eight hour window in which to effect changes prior to the second race. The gear ratio was reduced from 3.15 to 2.95, and a one hundred pound weight was added near the rear transom. A Holley carburetor was installed as well.

The next race was a 'must win' race for the Canadian challenger if she wanted there to be a third and final race. Her chances were minimized by the media, based on what they had already seen:

> ….when a jumpy boat starts digging water; the driver must back off or turn over. Braden kept **Supertest** afloat and running to the finish. A probable truth is that **Supertest** lacked balance and Braden lacked sufficient hours on it to have the proper feel of the racer after its bottom was changed and its power plant switched.
>
> The grave weakness of the Canadian challenge all along has existed in the fact that the boat got all its test runs on the St. Clair River in Sarnia, while the man who was to drive her lived 150 miles away in Hamilton, Ontario. Braden, a bus company executive, could not 'live with the boat' he was to race. He had less hours on it than either Danny Foster, or Jim Thompson Jr. Foster, U.S. born, is ineligible to drive for Canada in the Harmsworth. Thompson Jr. has no racing experience, though he has driven in it as fast as Foster in test runs. (37)

The <u>London Free Press</u> provided this optimistic assessment: "Unless something in the way of a king-sized miracle occurs, Canada's chances of taking the coveted Harmsworth Trophy from the United States are slimmer than a toothpick after it has been sliced down the centre".(38)

The Second Race

On Monday, it appeared that a combination of rain and gusty winds would force the cancellation of the heat, but thirty minutes before the starting gun, the skies cleared up and the sun shone brightly. The race started some thirty minutes late, due to the U.S. Coast Guard being forced to clean up an accumulation of driftwood at the south end of the course. Bill Braden was desperate to have a fast start and get out in front of **Shanty**, but misjudged the starting time, and risked disqualification if he crossed before the starter's gun. He slowed the challenger to a crawl to gauge where **Shanty** was positioned. She was coming on fast, and even though the challenger crossed the line first, the American boat pulled into a quick seventy-five yard lead. By the end of the first lap, Colonel Schleeh's boat had a thirty-one second lead, and had set a Harmsworth lap record of 110.357 m.p.h. **Miss Supertest**'s first lap speed of 93.703 m.p.h. was the fastest lap she put out in the first two races. As **Shanty** entered the Belle Isle Bridge turn on the second lap, her engine died out and Russ Schleeh was forced to accept a tow back to the pits, ending his race day. Braden had until 7 p.m. to finish the race, and went around the course at a leisurely pace, never exceeding a speed of 90.827 m.p.h. on any one lap. Braden provided this view of what transpired:

> As I was coming out of the turn, I looked up expecting to see **Shanty**'s roostertail, and it wasn't there. I looked back as I hit the stretch on the Belle Isle side, and saw Russ bent down trying to get her going. I barreled along until I reached the upper turn…then I eased off….I knew then he couldn't catch me…even if he got started.(39)

Colonel Russ Schleeh offered this perspective in speaking to the author: "In the second race, we wanted to go as fast as possible and set a record that would stand for some time, but the spline driveshaft that powered the supercharger, broke….My thoughts were that we took a calculated risk, which didn't work….(40)

After the second race won by the Canadian challenger, Colonel Russ Schleeh, driver of the American boat Shanty, offers his congratulations to Bill Braden, under the watchful eye of Miss Supertest owner, Colonel Gordon Thompson.

The Supertest team was elated with the victory. It was the first Canadian boat to ever finish a Harmsworth race, and the first 'foreign' boat to win a victory since the triumph of Englishman Kaye Don in 1931.

Colonel Gordon Thompson, and his son Jim, share a victory handshake with Bill Braden, after the second race in the 1956 Harmsworth challenge.

The Third Race

Now it was all down to a 'winner take all' final race for the Harmsworth Trophy. It was held on Tuesday afternoon 28 August. The weather was once again the main story of the day. A full gale accompanied by winds of 60-70 m.p.h. basically ruined the three level judges stand sitting opposite the Detroit Yacht Club. Heavy tables and chairs were blown off of the dock, and a P.A. system sound truck had its horns and amplifiers ruined by the wind. The buoys, which marked out the course, had to be realigned. The start time was pushed back thirty minutes to 6 p.m. to allow a lake freighter, which was unloading coal at the Detroit Edison plant, to finish its task, so that it would no longer block off part of the upper turn. The International Race Commission had to decide to run the race or postpone it to another day. The Canadian representative was against a postponement, which it was felt would aid the American cause. The American representative was also for pushing on with the race.

Miss Supertest's only change on the day was a return to an alcohol based fuel. But the river remained turbulent. For the third straight race, Braden was the first to cross the starting line, but **Shanty** took the lead coming down the Belle Isle straightaway. The first lap turned out to be the fastest of the day, with the American boat at 97.869 m.p.h., and the Canadian boat three seconds behind at 96.672 m.p.h. As the laps passed, the American lead grew larger. After lap five, the gap was up to thirty-six seconds; and people on the shore could see Bill Braden's head lolling from side to side, as if he was going to fall unconscious. The Rolls Royce engine coughed and sputtered, and the prop kept coming out of the water. It appeared the engine was going to die out, and Braden had to back off on the accelerator. The gap between the two boats kept growing wider. By the end of the race, the differential was 2 ¼ miles. The winner posted an average speed of 89.750 m.p.h., while the Canadian boat averaged 83.756 m.p.h. When **Miss Supertest** crossed the finish line, it was to a cacophony of whistles and shouts from the parked yachts around the course: a testimony to the courage of Bill Braden for seeing the race to its conclusion, despite the cost to himself. The newspaper had this analysis:

> Bill was in a bad way. He had fainted or come close to it in the third lap, down near the bridge where **Supertest** all but stopped, but came to life again, when her pilot got himself under control. For the next 4 ½ laps, the 41 year old Braden, a slightly built man of only 150 pounds, fought nausea, fought his steering wheel, fought his foot throttle, and fought to finish a race he had no chance to win after the first lap, when he was only three seconds behind.

> **Shanty** got the checkered flag to the sound of sirens, whistles, cheers, and all the hurrah deserved by boat and pilot for keeping the international trophy in the country. **Supertest** also received applause more deserved than understood at the time as the checkered flag fell when it finally crossed the Parkview finish line. Braden headed for the pits at Kean's. He was half conscious, somewhat delirious. 'It's the fumes, the fumes' he was gasping. (41)

Braden stayed in the boat's cockpit until the regatta physician arrived. The doctor pronounced him to be in a state of shock, and a police ambulance was called to transport him directly to Jennings Memorial Hospital. There he was examined by a specialist, who wrote in his report:

> On 28 August 1956, I examined William Braden at Jennings Hospital, at the request of Dr. Ralph Johnson. The patient was alert and cooperative, but appeared

quite exhausted. He had difficulty in carrying out simple tests, as finger to nose and heel to knee tests. This was apparently on the basis of general fatigue. Except for general fatigue, no positive neurological signs were elicited. ...It is my impression that Mr. Braden is suffering from exhaustion syndrome. There was no objective evidence of carbon monoxide poisoning, the question of which came up because of lack of ventilation in the confines of the **Supertest** cockpit. I believe the patient should be treated with oxygen inhalation, and should be further observed.... (42)

Colonel Gordon Thompson provided his assessment to the President of the American Power Boat Association:

....the boat has not been an easy one to drive, calling for the need of a good deal of stamina....When we installed the stacks, very careful consideration was given to the possibility of monoxide, and it was determined that there was no liability in this respect....Verbally the Doctor reported that Bill Braden's incapacity was due to extreme exhaustion brought about from the strain and very rough ride he had taken in the final heat of the Harmsworth. One thing that may be detrimental to some drivers is the noise factor. (43)

After the presentation of the Harmsworth Trophy, the American team headed off to the hospital to join the Thompsons and Mrs. Braden at the bedside of the Canadian driver. Colonel Schleeh spoke these words to Bill Braden: "I'm very sorry Bill. You are the most courageous driver I have ever seen, and I consider it a privilege to have raced against you". (44)

Gordon Thompson had these words for Bill's uncle, Harry Greening: "Bill had a rough ride indeed, and no one could have done better with the boat than he did the way she was set up. It is our belief, Harry, that the boat had more power at the propeller, than any man could ride or control at the throttle.... (45)

Ted Jones, the designer of **Shanty**, and the most sought after boat builder in the county, had this to say:

With the proper boat and the motor (Rolls Royce) they have developed, I am sure the Thompsons could set all time speedboat records....There is nothing to compare with that motor they are using, but I am sorry to say the boat has faulty design....If there ever was a driver, it's Bill Braden. That man has got what it takes. (46)

The American newspapers praised **Shanty** and her driver, but the headlines focused on the individual bravery of Bill Braden. Writing a column entitled "Canadian Driver Proves Champ Losing Harmsworth", George Van of The <u>Detroit Times</u> said:

> If the Harmsworth was a test of motors then Bill Braden had the biggest one in the race. And that motor was Bill Braden's heart. But Bill came out of the third heat yesterday, a champion. What's a champion? He's the guy who has that extra little bit that wins. With Bill, it was a little bit more. Bill did all these things to the point of complete exhaustion, physical as well as mental. The race ended with Bill in Jennings Hospital.
>
> And Russ Schleeh was there. So were the Waggoners and the owners of Bill's boat, J. Gordon Thompson and son, Jim. And so were a lot of others who understood what Bill had done in keeping **Miss Supertest** going long after the point of no return in physical stamina. They were there because they wanted to be there to admire the thing called 'guts' in sports, a sheer, raw display of magnificent courage.
>
> Had there been a veiled insinuation that Bill lacked the courage after losing the first heat Saturday? Canadian friends said it had happened. It obviously became a cruel, grinding hurt inside Bill which the triumph in the second heat Monday did little to assuage….Bill Waggoner, whose **Shanty I** won the trophy, was magnanimous in his admiration: 'I don't see how you did it. I was worried about you. I saw you duck into a couple [of waves] that would have made me quit….'
>
> Jim Thompson aboard his rescue boat went out looking for Bill, mired in the river traffic, after the race. 'When he saw us, he collapsed' J. Gordon Thompson said. 'He was bushed when you saw him stop after the third lap…but he kept **Supertest** going the rest of the way on guts alone'.
>
> In the hospital after his clothes were cut off, Bill was murmuring: 'I did a bad job'. His wife, at his side, was telling him he was wrong: 'You did a good…a wonderful job'. Bill had done what no driver since Gar Wood in 1920…had done…finish all three heats…make the Harmsworth a boat race.…It was the best of all Harmsworth's here and the best motor of all was Bill Braden's heart.(47)

Realistically, could **Miss Supertest** have hoped to win the 1956 Harmsworth competition? The American team did not feel that they could be beaten. Russ Schleeh had these observations some four decades after the races:

Our team had a high degree of confidence going into the race....During the second heat of the Harmsworth. I did not feel that the **Supertest** boat was very competitive since it appeared to be handling so poorly....There was no questions that we had the best riding boat, which allowed for higher speeds....I wasn't concerned with the start of the race, as I felt we could later pass the **Supertest** boat because of the superior handling quality of the **Shanty**....I had nothing but admiration for Bill Braden. Nobody could have driven that boat any better than he. I drove beside him after the first turn of the Third Heat, and saw the terrible beating he was taking, and was concerned for his safety. (48)

Race observers felt that it was only a matter of time in each race that the Americans, with the faster boat, would burst into the lead. Canadians felt that the constant repairs to the boat in the week prior to the race, put the challenger off balance, and over the three days never raced to her potential. But she had put up a better performance than any Harmsworth challenger had done on American waters....

Bill Braden was kept in hospital overnight for observations. He was released on the following day in an improved enough condition to drive his own car back to Waterdown. He would never drive an unlimited class hydroplane again, being replaced on the Supertest team by American Danny Foster, and then later, by his friend, Art Asbury.

Chapter 7: One Last Race

As noted earlier, in 1902, Mr. Alfred Harmsworth, later to become Lord Northcliffe, the proprietor of the <u>Daily Mail</u>, and other publications, chose to present a trophy to give support to the development of the motor launch, which at the time was sagging behind the motor car in prestige. It was to be a contest between gentlemen, and was to be run offshore. It was open to all the countries in the world. It would become recognized as the world symbol of supremacy in motor boat racing. It was presented to the Automobile Club of Great Britain and Ireland to serve as trustees. The first race for the Trophy was held in 1903.

By 1924, it was recognized that the prohibitive cost of building hydroplanes to compete for the British International (Harmsworth) Trophy emphasized the necessity of producing a new trophy for a class of boat which could be built for a moderate sum of money (@L300-700).

His Royal Highness, the Duke of York, who would later become King George VI, consented to associate himself in an active manner with the promotion of a trophy by racing boats of this type. This was the only Royal trophy in existence for powerboat racing; and the only trophy donated by British royals. The trophy was the world's most expensive power boating award, costing $10,000. It depicted a winged figurine flying over a boat in a sea of pure gold, all on an ebony stand.(1) At the outset, the engines in the competing boats were limited to a capacity of 1 ½ liters, and this class was held until 1930, when it was changed to a 3 litre (standard) engine. This class was returned until 1938 when the rules were again changed to a fuel allowance formula of 7 ¾ imperial gallons per heat, there being no restriction on engine size.

The first race was in 1924 at Torquay, England, when French and British boats competed. The next race was held in 1926 on the River Thames when the U.S., Canada, France, Germany and the British all sent contestants. Harry Greening was there as a competitor with his **Rainbow V.** Unfortunately, he ran into a mattress that was floating in the Thames, and the damage forced him out of the race. In 1927-1928, the race was moved to Southampton, and back to the River

Thames, when both the Americans and the British challenged for it. The final pre-World War II race was held in 1938 at Torquay, England, when the British, Americans and Canadians matched racing hulls; and the American, S. Mortimer Auerbach came home with the trophy after driving his **Emancipator VII** to victory. Ironically, Will Braden and his parents were on a European trip, and were in Torquay for the race. He had a photo album replete with 8 x 10 photos of all the boats in the race.

The distance for the race had been set at 90 nautical miles, in a series of three heats. The Trophy was awarded to the country of the boat obtaining the highest aggregate of points. The Americans had garnered the trophy in 1927, 1929, and 1938.

The most recent competition had been held at Lake Windermere in England in 1951, when Art Hatch of Hamilton, Ontario, in his boat **Costa Livin**, had brought the trophy to Canada. It marked the first occasion that a Canadian had ever won a British motor boat trophy. Because of its construction of solid goal, Hatch had great difficulty in getting the permission of the British Government to bring it back to Canada. During its stay in Canada, the trophy was insured for $7500, and was kept by the Canadian Boating Federation. (2)

In early 1958, the Canadian Boating Federation applied to the Marine Motoring Association of Great Britain for their permission to stage the race in Canada. When Royal Assent was provided by the Queen Mother, the sanction was awarded to the Huntsville Boating Association, which would conduct the race. Conditions of the race allowed acceptance of as many as five entries from any one country. In order to eliminate boats of the unlimited class from competing, only 12 ½ gallons of 87 octane gasoline were allowed to each boat per thirty nautical mile heat.

Rules called for a maximum field of five entries from each competing country, although it was not a team race. Each boat competed on its own, with the trophy going to the boat that gained the most points over the three heat, ninety nautical miles race. In each heat, scoring was based on 4 points for the winning boat, 2 points for a second place, and one point for being third. In the event of a tie on points at the end of the race, the trophy would be awarded to the boat averaging the highest aggregate speed throughout the three heats.

There were five boats from the United States that were challenging in the hopes of taking the trophy back south of the border. They included **Suddenly**, driven by Bud Schroeder from Niagara Falls, New York; and Joe Albee's **Sir Ron II** from Dearborn, Michigan. Albee was a 35 year old, with eight years experience driving racing boats. As well, there was **Tyree** driven by Joseph Tate, also from Dearborn, and Harold Bucholtz's **Too Bad** From North Tonawanda, near Buffalo. Finally, Bob Schroeder, also from Niagara Falls was driving **Wahoo**. The Canadian Boating Federation had chosen the following five boats as defenders of the Duke of York Trophy:

Huntsville's Art Asbury was driving **Miss Muskoka**; Bill Hodgson's **Miss Canadiana** (formerly **Miss O'Keefe**) came up from Weston; Chuck Irish from Hamilton brought his **Cheetah;** Dave Carter drove the Toronto based boat **Doo-de-Doo**, and finally Bill Braden's **Ariel V.**

Bill Braden, Art Asbury and Chuck Irish, three of the five Canadian drivers who would defend the Duke of York Trophy against five American competitors on Fairy Lake near Huntsville on the last weekend of August 1958.

This race was to be the first serious competition for **Ariel V.** Braden had purchased her in 1954, while he was working with **Miss Supertest.** She was burned in a fire and had to be rebuilt. Braden had raced her previously in a local race at Port Carling against less than severe competition. In a radio interview done by Art Asbury in the Braden kitchen, in an attempt to boost public interest in the race, Braden expressed enthusiasm for the layout of the course, which was a triangular course providing three turns per lap, instead of the normal two turns which would occur with the traditional 1 2/3 mile rectangular course that usually was laid out on this body of water. (3)

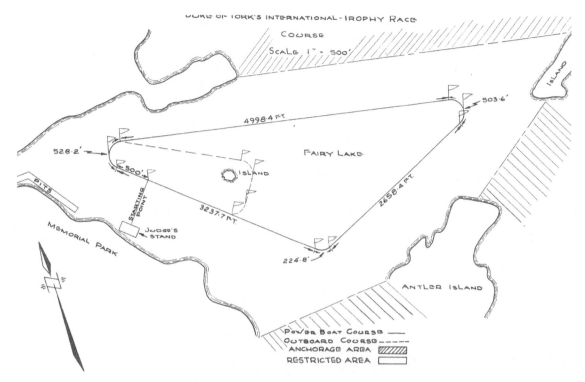

The layout of the Duke of York race course on Fairy Lake, Huntsville.

On Saturday 30 August, Heat #1 was held, as the third racing event of the day's program. It was a heat of fifteen times around the two mile triangular course on Lake Fairy at Huntsville. By the end of the heat, only Art Asbury had gained any points for Canada: attaining one point for his third place finish. A series of mechanical failures had put three of the five Canadian boats out of action during the race. Bill Hodgson's boat had led the field for the first four laps until, unfortunately, in lap #5, he broke a drive shaft. On the same lap, Chuck Irish pulled out with a defunct magneto. On the eighth lap, Bill Braden was pressing **Too Bad** for the lead. But the connecting hose from **Ariel V**'s water scoop came loose. Braden replaced it but could not get the engine to restart. This left the American boat **Suddenly** in undisputed possession of second place, and that is how it stayed until the end of the race, with the winner posting a time of 32 minutes, 41.9 seconds. The final standings for Heat #1 were: 1st **Too Bad**, 2nd **Suddenly,** 3rd **Miss Muskoka,** 4th **Sir Ron II**, 5th **Tyree** and 6th **Doo-de-Doo**. Both Bill Braden and Chuck Irish received a D.N.F. (4)

Heat #2 was scheduled to be run on the Sunday from 12:30-1:15 pm as the first event of the day. The Canadians knew that unless they captured all three podium positions in the second heat, that their chances of holding on to the Duke of York Trophy were nonexistent.

Bill Braden checks his watch before taking Ariel V out on Fairy Lake
for the last race of his life on Sunday August 31st.

Right from the start, it was going to be a dog fight. Bud Schroeder in **Suddenly** set a hot pace from the outset. He was closely followed by **Ariel V,** with **Sir Ron II** and **Miss Canadiana** right behind at the end of the first lap. But there had been a problem right at the outset. Between the firing of the one minute gun and the starting gun, **Cheetah** and **Sir Ron II** had inadvertently crossed the starting line, and then returned back to start with the rest of the field. But they were disqualified by that early start. However, with the boats so closely bunched together at the end of each lap, it was impossible for the race officials to flag the disqualified boats off of the course successfully, due to the flying spray and engine noise.

As the boats approach the starting line for the ill-fated second heat, Joe Albee's Sir
Ron II leads the pack, while Ariel V is in fifth place at the very left.

Wahoo limped off to the pits after one circuit of the course, and **Ariel V** sought to overtake the leader, Bud Schroeder, while Bill Hodgson slipped past **Sir Ron II** on the second lap. By the end of that same lap, Hodgson had moved into second place. In the third lap, the jockeying for position had continued. **Too Bad** had passed both **Ariel V** and **Sir Ron II** to take over third place behind leaders **Suddenly** and **Miss Canadiana**. Bob Finlayson, in his written analysis of the race, noted that "....the pace was torrid with every boat ready to take advantage of the slightest opportunity, if provided, to pass his nearest rival...."(5)

Joe Albee in his Sir Ron II prior to the fatal crash with Ariel V.

Then came the fateful fourth lap, the events of which can best be described in the words of Art Asbury, who was the only other observer to what transpired:

[At the time of the accident, Asbury was in 5th place and more than 200 feet behind the two boats] I had decided to let the two of them fight it out for third and fourth place, and had made up my mind to make my bid to take the race in the tenth lap [2/3 of the way through the fifteen laps]. I throttled down to 75 or 80 mph as I hit the first of the three buoys not too bad. While I was making a turn of the first buoy, **Ariel** and **Sir Ron II** were racing around the third and final buoy of the turn.

There was probably not much more than ten feet between them, and I believe **Ariel V** was in the lead as they turned the last buoy. **Sir Ron II** was on the inside, and Braden and **Ariel V** was outside of him. As **Ariel V** took the corner, from what I saw, it nearly tipped over. It's too bad it hadn't, for I believe Bill Braden would have been alive, had he been flung from his boat.

When I came past the third buoy, I noticed **Sir Ron II** slowing and coming to a stop in the water, with **Ariel V** wedged onto the hull of **Sir Ron II**. They were about one hundred feet down the stretch past the final buoy of that turn. The driver of **Sir Ron II** was pointing to a spot back by the final buoy of the turn, Asbury said, and he guided the boat to the point, I knew he was trying to direct me to where Bill Braden was.

I became frantic trying to find him, and I felt he would be unconscious, and realized the life jacket he was wearing would not float an unconscious person so his face would be out of the water.

I did not see Braden until I got ten feet from him, and then I recognized his helmet in the water, but it didn't look as though there was anyone under it. All I could see was torn pieces of his lifejacket collar. The color of the water around the helmet indicated he was bleeding and seriously hurt. He was floating face downwards.

I stopped **Miss Muskoka** and dived in. I was alone. I reached him and lifted his face from the water, and when I touched his chest with my other hand, I realized what I feared worst had happened to a great friend, and without a doubt the finest gentleman that Canada has ever known....(6)

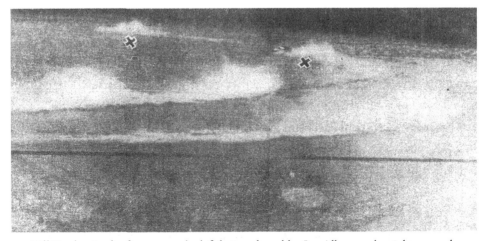

Bill Braden in the far turn at the left being chased by Joe Albee, at the right, seconds before their fatal crash on Fairy Lake, on Sunday 31 August 1958.

The accident had not been witnessed from either the judges' barge or the pit area with some 3500 fans on hand, because of the positioning of the island in the lake, which blocked out sight of that distant turn at the far end of the course. Before race officials were able to flag down the leading boats, while Asbury was in the water, the boats roared past him two more times, and he could have been caught in their churning propellers. But Asbury had thought only of saving his friend of the past ten years: the man whose friendship and support had help raise him to the top level in the race boat world. But he was too late….An official patrol boat, positioned on that turn, was alongside in a couple of minutes. Braden was taken aboard the boat, and the regatta doctor pronounced that he had died instantly. After Bill Braden's body was taken aboard the patrol boat, Art Asbury climbed back into his green hulled boat, and raced across the course to the official starting barge. He zoomed in, cut his motor, and tersely announced to the race officials: "Bill Braden's dead". That was the first inkling the larger boating community had of the tragedy that had occurred a few minutes earlier.

An investigation showed that **Ariel** was a few feet ahead going into that far turn. The boat swung wide on the turn; while Albee turned his boat sharply into the area between the buoy and the Canadian boat. The **Sir Ron II** made a sliding turn, but as **Ariel** straightened out of its turning momentum, the American boat climbed up on her port side, and the American's propeller ripped its way along **Ariel's** port deck and cockpit, knocking the Canadian driver out of the boat and into the water. Death had been almost instantaneous, as Braden's chest had been ripped open by the prop, and the life preserver had kept him from sinking in the lake. **Ariel V** was badly damaged on the port side, and the cockpit padding had been torn into shreds. The boat remained afloat upside down, and was later towed to a nearby dock area where a crane lifted her out of the water.

Coroner Doctor J.P. Davies aided by O.P.P. Constables Frank Geall and Ian Hutcheson conducted an on the spot investigation of the accident immediately afterwards. He concluded based on damage to **Ariel V** that the two boats were close together on the turn and the starboard sponson of **Sir Ron II** mounted the port sponson of Braden's craft. Cuts on **Ariel's** decking as well as bent pipes on the port side of her motor supported this theory. It was believed that as the American boat's sponson shifted off the Canadian boat that her propeller swung inwards towards the stern and the driver's seat, with Bill Braden trapped in it. Braden saw the threat it posed, and attempted to fend it off. This view is supported by an examination of Braden's body, which showed that part of the left hand had been lopped off. The padding behind Braden's seat had been chewed up, and a piece of **Ariel's** transom (tail) had been cut off. Her port bow decking had been damaged extensively as well. Dr. Davies added the following noteworthy detail:

> ….a piece of his [Braden's] coveralls found on the propeller shaft of **Sir Ron II**
> indicated to the investigators that the American boat's propeller had probably
> become entangled in Braden's clothing, cutting his chest deeply and carrying him

from his cockpit into the water, where the propeller action flung his body free. The damage to the driver's chest was extensive, and he wouldn't live little more than a minute or two…Dr. Davies believed considering the extensive loss of blood. (7)

The Coroner believed that **Ariel V** was running at a very low speed at the time of the collision as Braden was straightening her out after a long buffeting battle in choppy waters around the buoys at the far turn.

No blame was affixed for the accident. Bob Finlayson as Commodore of the Canadian Boating Federation stated: "It's an accident that has only about one chance in a million of happening. Racing boats go around turns like this every day. They nudge each other and nothing happens. It couldn't happen again in a million years."(8). Despite being absolved of any responsibility for the accident, Joe Albee was devastated. He was taken to the Huntsville Memorial Hospital where he was given sedatives. Later he said: "I lunched with Bill before the race; that doesn't make it any easier either."(9) Art Asbury was in shock, and was taken to the same hospital, where he was sedated and kept overnight for observation. Braden's mechanic, Gil Zamprogna, broke down and wept in the pits on hearing the news. Harold Bucholtz, was so grief stricken that he also required medical attention.

The drivers got together and held a meeting soon after, voting not to go on with the race. Drivers of the other classes of boats agreed, and the whole schedule of races were called off. An even greater tribute was paid by the American drivers, who voted to a man, along with their Canadian counterparts, to ask the Canadian Boating Federation to engrave Bill Braden's name on the Duke of York Trophy as the 1958 winner.

It was announced soon after that the Duke of York Trophy would be awarded posthumously to Bill Braden: "The widow of the driver…will be awarded a personalized trophy and her late husband's name will be engraved on the original cup. The winner of the heat…was Harold Bucholtz….He asked the trophy be awarded to Mrs. Braden, in memory of the driver 'who gave everything'". (10)

After a young man dies unexpectedly in the prime of his life, it is always interesting to hear his eulogies from the people who knew him on a daily basis. In Bill Braden's case, these people were the newspaper writers who had followed his career on a regular basis over the years. Harry Eisen was the longtime boating columnist of the London Free Press:

> Platitudes are a dime a dozen in the sports world. Most of them are just words of praise that are usually forgotten 24 hours later as some new star zooms across…
> but when such phrases as 'a real sportsman', 'a fine courageous gentleman' were

applied to Bill Braden, they fit. And he wore them well. Because Braden WAS a real sportsman and a fine courageous gentleman.

Braden's tragic and untimely death came as a numbing shock to many people who knew him. Bill made many friends here during the four year period he drove Jim Thompson's Miss Supertest. There was nothing artificial about Braden. Everyone liked him instinctively.

This writer, through covering Miss Supertest's trials and tribulations since she was first launched…came to know Braden well. He was always soft spoken and smiling. In fact, we fail to recall even one occasion when Bill was anything but his usual cheerful self. Many a time before or after a race, when most speedboat drivers hid away from reporters…Braden was most co-operative. He wasn't seeking publicity either. Braden wasn't that type. He was merely being what he always was…a nice guy. (11)

Ivan Miller was a scribe for the <u>Hamilton Spectator</u>, and had these observations of the man:

It might have been a 'one in a million' tragedy that took the life of speedboat racing's better known enthusiasts, but it was nonetheless a mishap that brought mourning to countless friends, associates, competitors, and admirers, for Bill typified the sport that was his first love.

He came by his enthusiasm for speedboats naturally, for his uncle…made history with his famous 'Rainbows' in another era, and in many ways, Bill exceeded the exploits of his illustrious uncle because he was concerned with a newer, faster type of craft, and indeed, had piloted **Miss Supertest** to a Canadian record of 154 mph, a speed well in excess of the potentialities of the craft, in his famed uncle's time.

Bill was not only a racing driver; he was a designer and an engineer of international repute. The boat in which he lost his life was the fifth of the **Ariel** line, a sixteen foot heavily powered craft, capable of well over 100 mph, and it had just been rebuilt, and was being raced for the first time since.

As a matter of fact, the late Bill Braden raced to a world's championship with the first of the **Ariel** line, about ten years ago, and in 1951, with the **Ariel IV**, he was the first man to exceed 100 mph with an inboard motor in such a small craft.

We have said that his reputation as an engineer, driver and designer was international. So was his wide circle of friends. No one ever found him anything but kindly and courteous. Newsmen were 'solid' on him because he was never too busy to take time out and offer full explanations of everything connected with his boats and racing. His sportsmanship was apparent in all his activities and he was an individual who never lost, for a second, an intense enthusiasm and a burning desire to excel.

There will be many nice things said about Bill for a long time to come, but nothing nicer than a defeated rival once exclaimed: 'He's the finest chap in the world to know and race with'.(12)

The following editorial appeared in the Hamilton Spectator:

We can say little about William Greening Braden, an able and popular young businessman of this city, who was killed in a tragic boating accident near Huntsville on the weekend, without feeling the tribute inadequate. Life was good to him, and yet in a sense it was the way he carried his good fortune and charm that made him so universally and profoundly liked. Bill Braden was a gentleman, and as so many young men who die in war and peace too soon, and leave little on the public annals, are gentlemen. We like to think he typified, rather than uniquely represented, the best in Canadian manhood. The sympathy of his host of friends and associates will be with his family in the bereavement. (13)

The Sports Department at the Spectator went on to offer this eulogy:

….An intense and curious person. Mr. Braden had many facets to a bright and distinguished career. Power boating successes were only a few of his accomplishments, but they were the most publicized.

Overseas where he latterly held the rank of Major in a R.C.E.M.E. group, he was also one of the best motorcycle riders. Despite his intensity and his busy rounds, he was a gentlemanly, dignified person who reserved for the hazardous sphere of boat racing, his fierce bent for competition. In boat racing, he preferred the competitive race to the straight run over a measured distance.

He had an affection for all sports, many of which he was able to share with his family.…He enjoyed the interest of young people in all his undertakings. He had allotted time in his busy schedule to follow the activities of students at Hillfield, T.C.S., McMaster and McGill, all of which he attended.

....His clubs included the Hamilton Club, Thistle Club, Tamahaac Club, Officers Institute, Hamilton Power Boat Association, and Canadian Boating Federation....(14)

Finally George Van was a regular boating writer for the <u>Detroit Times</u>, and contributed the following poignant piece:

Bill Braden, who went out of this life, racing his boat at Huntsville, didn't keep his word. Two years ago, he said he was through. He had quit. He said this as he lay in the hospital on Cadillac Avenue. His racked frame was bruised and battered from ankle to chin. Carbon monoxide fumes had come close to completing Bill's story that afternoon in the river.

Miss Supertest... was a wild, unpredictable thing as Bill raced her against Colonel Russ Schleeh with **Shanty**....The wonder of it all that day was that Braden even took a heat. Certainly it was more Braden than **Supertest**.

Thompson picked Braden for the job because he was Canada's finest driver. The rest of the daredevils who pilot these unlimited bombs will tell you he was as good as any on either side of the border.

That night at the hospital is sort of unforgettable in memory. Braden came out of a coma, and was apologetic for not having done better. People in the room, and they included Thompson, Bill Waggoner, who owned **Shanty** and Schleeh were stirred to the point of tears by the words of this gentlemanly and gallant driver.

Yesterday, Schleeh said: 'He was the bravest and most courageous sportsman I've known'. Thompson [said]: 'There was never a man with more heart than Bill. It was almost frightening the way he wanted to win the Harmsworth. It seemed as if he felt responsible for the honor of the Dominion in racing. He gave more than was asked'.

Leonard Thompson, custodian of the Harmsworth Trophy in America and an active official since the early 20's paid this tribute: 'He always wanted to represent the Maple Leaf with the glory that surrounded his uncle'.

That's another reason why he came out of retirement to race for the Duke of York Trophy with his 266 **Ariel** last Sunday. There was also the urge to drive. Older drivers know this....

Bill Braden had one motor that had more power than any of the engines he handled, even Supertest's Rolls-Royce Merlin.

That would be Bill Braden's heart.... (15)

Finally there was a very touching obituary in the T.C.S. <u>Record</u>:

Bill Braden's death on Sunday August 31 came like a bolt from the blue; he was the innocent victim of an unprecedented accident in a power boat race. For many years Bill had excelled as a racer of motorboats; in 1939 he won a World's Championship at the Canadian National Exhibition and from then on he made records year after year....

W.G. Braden came to T.C.S. in 1929 and left in 1933. He was a bright spark in any group and the dull hours were few when Bill was about. A good athlete, he played on the hockey team and the second football team....

Bill was always ready to help any worthwhile cause, and he was a most loyal Old Boy being President of the Hamilton Branch of the O.B.A. He had been Chairman of the Board of Hillfield School, and he liked to have young people around him. In recent years we had seen much of him for he often visited the School with his charming family to see his son, John. The memory of Bill Braden will never grow dim. (16)

And what about the Braden family who were in attendance at the weekend's race, as they were at all of Bill's races throughout his career? Bill Jr. recounted how his Dad had spent the week in Sarnia setting up the bus line there, which was set to go into operation on the following Tuesday after Labor Day. Young Bill had been working with a threshing crew on a farm, and on the Friday received two phone calls, one from his father, and the other from the housekeeper, advising him to be ready to depart for Huntsville at 2 p.m. He was unsure as to why the departure time was so critical. It turned out that the Friday was Lakefair Day at the Canadian National Exhibition, with a planned parade of the boats, both Canadian and American that would be competing at Huntsville. The parade was scheduled to begin at 3:30 p.m. (17) Father and son drove to Toronto, where they hung around for a time. Bill Jr. noted that "nothing much was happening", nor did anything end up happening. So they then began the drive north towards Huntsville. Young Bill, who had been driving a horse van on the farm, offered to drive the vehicle, knowing the strenuous week his father had experienced: "you must be tired...".(18) But his Dad said that he was OK, and continued to drive north.

Mom and the rest of the family had been staying at the family cottage on Milford Bay, one hour distant, throughout the month of August. His dad had been coming home on weekends, and had spent the first two weeks of August there on summer vacation. Bill recounts meeting him at the waterfront in mid-August as he was trying out **Ariel IV**. He remembers: "He asked me if I wanted to take the boat for a spin? This was the first time he had ever said this. Who was going to say 'no'? It was a surprise and I was excited. I took it out for a spin and brought it in...." (19)

On Saturday, Dad wanted to be in the pit area for 7 a.m., because the mechanics had switched the motor of **Ariel IV** into the new boat. After the boat had had her problems in the first heat, his Dad had commented: "I told Gil [Zamprogna] that we should check the motor. Gil said it was good. I think that was a mistake."(20)

On Saturday night, the mechanics worked with the staff of Edgar Riley's boat works, who Bill Sr. knew, to prepare the boat after its mechanical problems. They were at the pits area by 7 a.m. on the Sunday morning. Bill Jr. remembers his last conversation with his Dad: "He was getting ready to go out in his boat and he had his life jacket on. He then said to me: 'Is there anything you need or like? Can I get you a hotdog?' It caught me by surprise because it was time to be focused on the race."(21)

When reflecting on what happened in the next hour, Bill Jr. said: "We never ever assumed that anything would happen. It was safer racing a boat than going down the highway in a car. Other than Pop Cooper, I didn't know anyone else at the time that had died. He had had enough of unlimiteds. But he wanted to get back into shape..."(22)

To watch the Sunday race, the family was positioned on the cliffside behind the judges' stand. It was drizzling as well. Bill Braden Jr remembered the afternoon:

> A lot of family friends went to the race. Anyone with an interest in boating was there. There was quite a bit of hype about it. It was being promoted on the Huntsville radio station....The good thing was we couldn't see it. There wasn't a clue even after it happened. Of course, you never think that something will happen. The first clue was seeing Art Asbury coming across the infield in a straight line towards the judges' stand. Whoever was announcing said something, but we didn't hear exactly what was said. A boat then came by close to the shore with a man with a megaphone asking if Mrs. Braden was there. A gentleman came over and she was taken away, and we saw a couple of rescue boats come into the pit area....We walked to the pits and were taken by a rowboat to a cottage across the mouth of the river, where mother already was. They offered us hot chocolate. We realized we did not know what was wrong. But she had seen him, and she told us what had happened. We were sitting on a couch, you are in denial and in shock.(23)

Bob Hutcheson, a thirty-one year old Huntsville man, whose 14 foot Mahone Bay molded plywood boat was being used by Commodore Bob Finlayson of the Canadian Boating Federation to get around the course, played a key role in the post-accident treatment of Mrs. Braden and her children. He recounted that once word got out about an accident, he and the Commodore went along the shoreline with a megaphone, calling for Mrs. Braden and the family to come to the shore's edge. They picked the whole family up in the boat, with no life preservers, and made their way to the dock area, where Bill Braden's body was being brought in on another boat. Joan Braden stepped off the boat and Mr. Hutcheson intercepted her, asking her where she was going. She said: "I'm going to help my husband". He told her to listen to him, and said: "There's nothing further you can do for your husband. Think of your children, they are going to need help". She stood erect, blinked her eyes once, and responded: "I understand what you've said" and turned back to be with their children. The boat ride continued across to the north side of the river, where Vice-Commodore Don Lough, had requisitioned a house where the family could spend some time grieving and composing themselves.(24)

Mr. Hutcheson gave these final thoughts to that eventful half-hour: "I've never seen a woman that I was more proud of or impressed with….I will never forget the composure and courage of Bill's wife, Joan".(25)

A damaged Ariel V being hoisted from Fairy Lake after the fatal crash.

Bill Braden Jr continued with his memories of leaving Huntsville and heading back to the family cottage:

> When we left, I was driving and instead of turning left towards Milford Bay, we turned right and went looking for the boat along the shoreline. We found it on its carrier. The back of the boat was missing. When we got back to Milford Bay, Francis Farwell was there and said: 'Over and over again, I talked to Will and told him he shouldn't be doing this'. Everyone was in shock and really did not pay attention to him.(26)

Then it was time to head back to Waterdown:

> ….We drove from Milford Bay back to the house. We got there Monday. Then we started to hear the word 'funeral'. We had never been to a funeral before and did not know what to do. All his old school buddies and many others were there. There were no plans. All these people were coming into our driveway. They were coming in numbers to pay their respects. My brother [John] and I were walking up and down the driveway and thanking people for coming.(27)

The wake was held at the Braden house:

> Francis' [Farwell] wife [Bill's mother in law] was focused on tradition. My mother was hopeless, as you would expect. They started to get things together. On Tuesday, the body was brought back from Huntsville. He had a scar on his forehead and was missing an arm. I saw him and said: 'That's him but it's not him'.(28)

The funeral was to be held in Grace Anglican Church in the village of Waterdown. The family knew the Minister, Pat Noble, to whom Francis Farwell had given the use of a cottage on Milford Bay. As well, Joan Braden was a regular in the Church choir. The weather was good on the day. Bill remembers on the drive from the house to the church, seeing a one block line of employees from the Hamilton Street Railway Company, standing in respect. It turned out that the Company had offered free transport to any employee who wanted to attend the funeral. The Minister did most of the speaking during the service, and Bill does not remember any family member delivering a eulogy. He did remember that one of the hymns sung was 'Praise My Soul The King of Heaven'. After the funeral, Bill Braden was buried in the churchyard next door.

Bill Jr. shared one final story from this period:

At the end of the second week, we are living like hermits. We decide it'd be a good idea to go to a movie to do something. At this time, there were news shorts in addition to the movie. So there was this report on the accident. We left the movie and did not stay to see it. I had been enrolled into OAC. By mid-September, I'm boarding in Guelph and came home on weekends. We did go north skiing at Christmas, and at that time, we started to carry on again.(29)

Chapter 8—Anecdotes

He was the kind of guy who would sit up all night and help you fix your boat so you could beat him in the races next day. (Art Asbury)

He was a very gentle sort of man, quite tall and thinner. He was very nice and very warm (Jim Thompson)

Will was very good looking. (Dorelle Cameron)

It was an interesting family: Aunt Margaret took flying lessons, and owned one of the first Ford V-8s in Hamilton. She wasn't healthy when she was young: she was quite delicate. Grandpa [Norm Braden] shot skeet at the Tamarac Club, but he was an avid golfer. He had to go to Pittsburgh frequently, and he always took his golf clubs with him. (Harcourt Bull)

I sensed that even with having attended school in Switzerland, and having had a glamorous childhood, he treated everyone the same. He used to visit a carpenter in Waterdown, whose daughter was in my class at school. His name was Ken. On the side of his truck was 'C' for 'Carpenter', so Dad used to call him 'CKen' [sken]. When they used to get together to talk about a project, there was no difference between them: they were a team working together on the project. (Gwyn Braden)

The entry to the Hamilton Street Railway bus depot was located at 18 Wentworth Street, and was 120 feet x 80 feet in width to be able to handle the buses. There was a parking area inside for the administration, and their vehicles were always washed, so Dad always came home with a clean car. (Bill Braden Jr)

He was never bossy to Gil Zamprogna (his boat mechanic). There was nothing bossy in his nature. Your social station in life was irrelevant to him. The fact that there was a group of uniformed bus drivers, lining the walkway from the church to his gravesite, was a mark of the respect that they had for him. (Norm Braden)

I never saw him gloomy….He had a very good sense of humor. (Harcourt Bull)

One Sunday I went with Dad to the Hamilton Street Railway office, where he had to verify the amount of money collected from the change boxes. I remember that there was a big pot full of change. (Dave Braden)

Dad said that once during the war, the jeep he was in got into an accident. They were sliding along the road upside down, and all that separated Dad from the road's surface was the jeep's tarpaulin roof. Dad said all that they would have had to do was to hit a pothole, and he would have had a broken back….(John Braden)

Dad was a very cautious person. There was an emergency bell in the basement if the furnace ever blew up, and we all had ropes in our bedrooms to be able to get out of the house if there ever was a fire. The fire extinguisher in the house was always up to date and had a sticker on it: He was a safety nut….(Norm Braden)

Mom used to get annoyed with Dad. On Sundays, she used to like going to Church, and expected him to be in the near proximity. The main dinner of the day was at noon. Most motorcycle racing was on Sunday at the time we were sitting down to Sunday dinner. The word 'race' had to be eliminated from the conversation, and was replaced by 'we're going to check out some "history"'(Bill Braden Jr)

I was one of a group of girls who had gone up to Moon River for the weekend. The news came over the radio that Mr. Braden had been killed and 'decapitated.' It was not a very pleasant ride back to Hamilton. (Betty Leggett, H.S.R. Switchboard Operator)

I bought my first motorcycle at age 14, and Dad's response insinuated 'that's not what you should be buying'. A few days later, he got me a Sturgis bike from a Hamilton store. I was really too young to drive in competitions, but it was good experience, and Dad said he would talk to the organizers about my riding as a 'novice'. (Bill Braden Jr)

On Sundays, we usually went to Grace Anglican Church in Waterdown, which I think was largely Mum's idea-but the whole family would go on important occasions, filling an entire row. Before we fidgeted our way through a long sermon, I vividly remember Dad once whispering to us, conspiratorially, that the best way to pass the time was to stare at some lady's hat (women always wore hats to church in the fifties) in one of the pews ahead of us, and if we all stared hard at the same hat, the sheer intensity of our stare would force her to turn around. As Mr. Noble went on and on with his sermon, we (or certainly I and Dad, and no doubt the others) stared and stared, relentlessly, and then suddenly, SHE TURNED AROUND! Joy to the world! (Gwyn Braden)

I think he understood engines, though I am unsure he ever took an engine apart like I had to do….When you are in the wire business, you have to know about engines. (Harcourt Bull)

Once I had the opportunity of meeting Gar Wood. Wood would traditionally hold a very formal afternoon gathering at his place on the river in conjunction with boat racing. His house was immense! Dad would take me everywhere: I was part of his gear. He told Wood: 'I brought my son along'. Wood said to me: 'I have something to show you', and he walks me into a ballroom, which had pictures of all his achievements. There was a ramp that went right down to the water level so that he could climb into any one of his boats. When the butler came to interrupt him and call him back to the guests upstairs, Wood said to him: 'Are you not aware that I have a very important guest with whom I am having a discussion? He is the nephew of Harry Greening, and tell the guest he can wait….' (Bill Braden Jr)

It was ironic that Bill died the way he did. He was very conscious of safety. He used to talk about his home in Waterdown, which was located in an isolated area. He talked about how he made sure of escape routes for the family in case of a fire. (Frank Cooke)

I remember Dad buying me my first two pigeons [ultimately he would own thirty-one of them]. (Dave Braden)

In 1957 when the family went to Europe on their trip, I was sent to camp. I had to be the only girl in the camp who had aerogrammes with typewritten addresses on them to send letters to a London, England address, so that Dad could hear about what I was doing at camp. (Gwyn Braden)

Bill and I were treated differently [being the eldest children]. We went to the races in Detroit and stayed at the Whittier Hotel. We were taken to a lot of events. We ate dinner at home in the dining room with Mom and Dad. It was a formal occasion. Dad would come home from work and change from one shirt and tie into another. Norm and Gwyn were required to eat earlier, and they ate out in the kitchen or in the library. They were allowed to bring their chairs as close as the swinging doors to the dining room….(John Braden)

He loved anything and everything mechanical. There were designs of boats and engines in many drawers around the house, and no doubt many more over in the 'boat shop' across the way. (Gwyn Braden)

One time, I was home in bed, sick, and Dad came in and started talking about a war story. He was in a strange place mentally….They were in a jeep, and enemy artillery shells started falling, and some fell near a tank just ahead. People started running away due to shell shock. We had to turn and get out of there. There were bodies laying around and we drove over some of them. I am pretty sure they were all dead….[was it a confession a decade later that he was still unsure whether they had all been dead?] (Norm Braden)

Dad would attend every running event [track and field] at summer camp if the children were involved. He attended because it was a competitive sport, and he loved competitive sports. (Bill Braden Jr)

When Hillfield moved out to Westdale, we'd go out there on weekends and play hockey. He played hockey, he played tennis, but he did not play golf. (Harcourt Bull)

I had a good friend…whose father was stern, stiff, aloof and rather scary. Another school friend's father was grumpy and fat. To me they belonged to a different universe from my own father, who was tall, friendly and very, very playful. When he came home from work, and took off his coat and hat to settle in for the evening, I remember feeling happy. He played the piano by ear, for fun, with lots of panache, and took great delight in skimming the notes of the whole keyboard for effect. He showed me how to dance the Charleston, which I thought was pure magic. At dinner, he would often have a trick or two up his sleeve-quite literally: he would put a nickel in the middle of his left palm, close his hand, and before you knew it, the nickel appeared in his right hand. Even in didactic mode, he was fun. Sitting up straight was important to him, and he encouraged us all to do it-imagining a string sticking straight up from the middle of the top of your head, and somehow being suspended from the ceiling. Then there was advice about earlobes: give them a nudge every once in awhile and they won't grow into pendulous lobes when you are old….(Gwyn Braden)

Dad had quite a few cars. He would say: 'I'm going to bring this car home to see if your mother would like it'. He had probably owned it for several months before he said this…. (Bill Braden Jr)

Dad felt quite comfortable working for his stepfather-in-law: he would not have cow-towed to him. He did not get bullied by him, and he was not beholden to him. He called him 'Francis' (Norm Braden)

Dad liked Trials riding on motorbikes. He built a Trials course behind the house for the children to navigate with their bicycles. It was used by the three eldest boys….

In the early 1950s, Dad and his good friend, Basil Southam, gave each other identical motorbikes as gifts, so they could explain to their wives that they had received it as a gift. This was not the first time that this happened: at the end of the war, they did the same thing with an automobile.

Some people who get into management become like little Hitlers. Bill liked to laugh: he did his job and expected people to do theirs. He was no overbearing Simon Legree. (Frank Cooke, Superintendent of Operations at the H.S.R., would later become Assistant G.M., and subsequently G.M.)

He was a gentle, fun-loving, seemingly contented person. I can't honestly ever remember him raising his voice or losing his temper, although I am sure he must have. There is no question in my mind that he loved his children and enjoyed each one of us….As far as I could tell, life revolved around us-and racing boats. (Gwyn Braden)

He divided his time between his passion (racing) and his family. (Harcourt Bull)

I think it's good to get Bill and John out….(Bill Braden's escape line when he wanted to get out of the house to go to a motorcycle race)

Dad was neat and consistent when it came to driving a motorbike. His feet never came off of the pegs. He would say: 'If I can get a good start…'

Dad always felt that it was the safest to drive on Highway 5 rather than the Q.E.W. He explained it was how the new highway was built, and the angles of vision were not the best. (Gwyn Braden)

I don't remember him ever falling off a motorcycle, nor getting in a boating accident (prior to 1958) (Bill Braden Jr)

Dad loved cars, and one time, he convinced the Administration that it was a good time to trade in his car (a Mercury station wagon).He had seen an Oldsmobile station wagon on a dealer's lot with a 375 h.p. engine, and once he got it, he used it to tow his boat around to races. (Bill Braden Jr)

Dad was a cautious driver: it was not like he needed to put his foot to the floor when he was not racing. Once he got in an accident on the new Q.E.W. In those early days, the Q.E.W. had cross streets that directly entered onto the highway. I was in the front seat and saw something and pointed it out to Dad: 'Look Dad look'. He took his eyes off of the road, and the car in front stopped, and there was an accident: as minor as possible. I felt partly guilty: he never said anything to me. (John Braden)

When he came home from work, it was 'family time'. If there had been a disagreement at work, the most he would say at home was 'I'm not in agreement', and he did not dwell on it any further. (Bill Braden Jr)

One time a visitor came to the McColl Farm, driving a red Allard, with a Cadillac V-8 engine, and told Dad to take it for a spin. Dad and Bill Jr. got in the front seat and Norman in the back seat. It was a mile uphill from the house to the entry to the property on the escarpment. Dad floored it and we were doing 50 m.p.h. uphill, as we hit the hairpin turn (20 m.p.h.) at the entry to the road. We tried to make the corner, but we spun around. It was the only time I ever saw him drive like that. (Norm Braden)

He liked to dance. (Harcourt Bull)

We always remember you at Rosey and hope to see you again someday….(Marguerite Carneol from Le Rosey in a letter to Bill Braden on 15 April 1948)

He took me for a ride in a Cadillac Allard: it was very fast and good for hill climbing: Dad's ability to go fast was beyond what I'd believe. He had been to race car tracks and to Indy. His cars were unique and not totally standard. He had a Jaguar SS in Europe: how did it get there? (Bill Braden Jr)

Was it nervousness that led him to be cautious? No he would not have raced if he was nervous. (John Braden)

Dad was very interested in all sports. He liked to be well dressed and have a sporty car: he was not the type of person you'd see in old coveralls. On a motorcycle trip, he would wear 'white ducks'. He never wore a sports shirt: he always had a tie. (Bill Braden Jr)

The love of my life was going out and shooting the BB gun with Dad. I was age 8. We are out and he listed the number of people who had been shot and killed with a BB gun. He demonstrated how to climb a fence carrying a BB gun, and how to look behind, and to the left and right. As he got off the fence, the gun went off and he got hit in the hand. He was shaking his hand and he said: 'You can't be too safe' (Norm Braden)

He was very popular at the Hamilton Street Railway. (Harcourt Bull)

Dad loved to take pictures-he was rarely without his camera, and I believe there is still a huge archive of 16mm films to prove it. He loved sporting events where families gathered-regatta, football and hockey games, school sports days. He had a most unusual set of sporty clothes that he would put on for special occasions: I am certain he had a pair of bright pink pants that he wore to the Star Island Regatta-I can even remember the dresser drawer they lived in. (This was a time when men did not wear pink pants!) (Gwyn Braden)

In the summer time we would enter the local canoeing races: we had enough family members to make a foursome in the canoe. We did 'reasonably well'. (Bill Braden Jr)

He was loyal to his friends from school and sports and the army and often told us about their lives. He loved stories: the kind you tell and the kind you read. I remember him telling me how much he enjoyed O. Henry and Ernest Thompson Seaton. He loved surprises: I remember his excitement once in hiding a new car-destined for Mum's birthday-in some bushes in Muskoka. Even at the time, young as I was, I had a sneaking suspicion that the car was more appealing to him than it would be to her! (Gwyn Braden)

Mom wanted a Georgian style house (in Waterdown). Dad was into structure with specific materials to be used. (Bill Braden Jr)

Dad played squash every week at the Thistle Club. He took the family skiing every weekend at the Ski Jump Inn in Huntsville as well as on the Christmas holidays. On Christmas Day, they would leave and travel north with another family, and spend the holiday there skiing. It was a steep hill with a rope tow powered by a Ford V-8 engine run by the Huntsville Ski Club. There were twelve to fifteen of us, and every hour that the lift operated, we kept the tow line running. In the evenings we played hockey on the ice rink.(Bill Braden Jr)

Yesterday I heard that Dad's picture was in the Hall of Fame at the C.N.E....His picture is beside [Prime Minister] Diefenbaker's. (Bill Braden Jr letter to his mother, 27 August 1961)

Your grandmother hired me when I had just started high school (age 14)....When your father was home, and we were in Waterdown, your mother and he would hold hands and walk around the property together....I spent very little time with your father. He did like to tease me gently because I was very shy. He loved his boat and loved to race it....he seriously considered buying the Duke Boat Company [located in Port Carling]...but decided against it....Your mother and he were very compatible and loving and close". (Carla Pruden letter to John Braden, 19 October 2009)

He was responsible for bringing the Duke of York Trophy Race to Canada. Everyone said: 'Will, you're too old. Everyone cautioned him not to race. He said 'I won't do it again'. His wife was quite nervous about him racing. (Harcourt Bull)

I admired the man from the time I first met him. He seemed to be a clean cut, intelligent, composed leader. I felt he was a perfect gentleman. I felt I was meeting a 'whole person'. Nearly always, you can see people are protecting something. He was not protecting anything. You felt you were meeting someone on equal terms. He struck you as a guy who had confidence in himself. (Bob Hutcheson)

With his Dad being at Westinghouse, they had an active travel itinerary, and they seemed to take trips in cars that exceeded a two week vacation. (Bill Braden Jr.)

All I can remember about Mr. Braden was that he was a very good looking man, well mannered, and treated his staff with respect. (Ruby Moore, retired H.S.R. employee)

We spent all our time together during working hours and would sometimes sneak out the back door for coffee so that Mr. Todd would not see us going (Frank Cooke)

He was tall and agile and blond haired: he was a man who was full of life. (Betty Leggett)

Endnotes

Chapter 1 Endnotes

(1) *Bill Braden Papers,* "Memorial Record of Distinguished Men of Indianapolis and Indiana-1912".

(2) <u>Ibid.</u>

(3) <u>Ibid.</u>

(4) <u>Ibid.</u>

(5) <u>Ibid</u>

(6) <u>Ibid.</u>

(7) <u>Ibid.</u>

(8) *Bill Braden Papers,* "Rotary Told Of Electrical Marvels", <u>Hamilton Spectator</u>, 2 February 1934.

(9) *Bill Braden Papers,* John R. Read, "Obituary", <u>Westinghouse Employees Magazine</u>, Volume 2 #8, October 1944, p. 2

(10) Bill Braden Jr. interview with the author, July 2009.

(11) *Bill Braden Papers,* N.S. Braden Letter to <u>Hardware in Canada</u> Magazine, 4 January 1933.

(12) *Bill Braden Papers*, B. Greening Wire Company Limited, "Wire, Its Manufacture, Antiquity and Relation to Modern Uses", December 1892.

(13) Vice-Commodore Colin Jacobs, R.H.Y.C. to the author, 24 September 2009.

(14) *Bill Braden Papers*, Harry Greening Obituary, <u>Hamilton Spectator</u>, 26 February 1960.

(15) *Bill Braden Papers*, "In The World Of Yachting", n.d.

(16) *Bill Braden Papers*, F.W. Horenburger, "Racing Against The Clock", <u>Motor Boating</u>, August 1956, p. 129.

(17) Bill Braden Jr. interview with the author, August 2009.

(18) *Bill Braden Papers*, F.W. Horenburger, "Gold Cup Racing As It Was In '24", <u>Motor Boating</u>, September 1956, @p. 45.

(19) *Bill Braden Papers*, George Bernard, "Harry Greening and his Rainbows", <u>Canadian Power Boating</u>, Summer 1929, pp.20-21.

(20) Harry Greening Obituary, <u>op.cit.</u>

(21) *Bill Braden Papers*. Having amalgamated with Donald Ropes and Wire Cloth Limited in 1963, it operated for years under the name of Greening Donald Company Limited in Orangeville, Ontario. Today that same company continues to exist, though now it is located 'off shore', and the author was unable to find its new name through study on the internet.

(22) Harry Greening Obituary, <u>op.cit.</u>

(23) *Bill Braden Papers*, Bill Braden to H.B. Rutherford, 31 July 1956.

Chapter 2-Endnotes

(1) <u>Hamilton City Directory</u>, 1910, p. 220.

(2) <u>Hamilton City Directory</u>, 1916, p. 307.

(3) Barry Wansbrough, <u>Echoes That Remain</u>, (Hamilton: Hillfield-Strathallan College, 2001), pp.10-14.

(4) <u>Ibid.</u>, pp. 31-44.

(5) <u>Hamilton City Directory</u>, 1924, p.395.

(6) Interview with the author, 8 February 2010.

(7) Surprisingly, the asthma left him alone during his years at Hillcrest and T.C.S. The next serious bout would not hit him until he was in Switzerland. His comments in his 'personal' diary was: "In June 1934 at Geneva, Switzerland. Got asthma quite badly. Due

I think to drinks (mostly beer) the night before. This was first reoccurrence for almost ten years". Braden was a meticulous keeper of personal data. In this 'diary', he noted that his weight fluctuated between 148 (1933) to160 (1938), and back down to 145 while he was overseas (1943); and then 149 in November 1955, followed by 154 in September 1956. He picked up a scar on his forehead in a T.C.S. hockey game at Pickering in 1931 when hit by a skate. He added a scar to his chin when hit by a Paul Metternich skate in a Le Rosey hockey practice in February 1934. A third scar came as a result of a #2 closer at the Greening Wire Company, hitting his lower lip, and knocking out a tooth. He had a variety of health issues, all of which were chronicled. He had pneumonia @1920, kidney issues in 1921 or 1922, whooping cough in 1922 or 1923, impetago in 1930, measles in 1935, his left ankle was dislocated in 1936, chicken pox in 1937, and strep throat in 1938.

(8)   *Bill Braden Papers,* "Rider of Promise", <u>Hamilton Spectator</u>, 22 October 1925.

(9)   *Bill Braden Papers,* "Thrills Provided At Hunt Club Show", <u>The Mail and Empire</u>, 8 January 1928

(10) Viola Lyons, Assistant Archivist at the J.D. Burns Archives at Trinity College School in explaining the concept of the 'Middle Remove' noted: "No concern for esteem building in those days....they really believed in being straight up.", Letter to the author 23 October 2009.

(11) <u>Trinity College School Record</u>, p. 30.

(12) <u>Trinity College School Record</u>, April 1933, p. 7.

Viola Lyons made the following observation: "So this would indicate that he left the school without having completed the full number of courses for the Ontario certificate. (Not entirely unusual in those days....)", Letter to the author 23 October 2009.

(13) Bill Braden Jr. interview with the author, August 2009.

(14) *Bill Braden Papers,* Newspaper Article, "Atterrissages Forces" .

(15) Barbara Stromstad, who works in the Alumni Department today at Le Rosey, wrote the following quote about marking in the 1930s: "At that time, the grades were out of 10, and they used to say that 10 was for God, 9 for a professor, and then on for students, so an 8 was a very good grade", Letter to the author 22 October 2009.

(16) <u>Echo de Rosey</u>, 1934, p.18.

(17) <u>Ibid.</u>, p.16.

(18) <u>Ibid.</u>, p. 17.

(19)   The <u>Echo De Rosey</u> assessed the weekend's activities with this quote: "The Pentecost Holiday, coming as it does right in the middle of the term, is a welcome break in the ordinary school routine. It affords three days of rest and relaxation before the last half term and the College Board Exams. The tennis tournament always excites a great deal of enthusiasm, and this year's series was no exception. Competition was keen and interest was high as the final rounds drew closer. The rowing, also this year, added a great deal of excitement to the holidays, and it was with a great deal of regret that we went back to our studies on Tuesday morning".

(20)   <u>Ibid.</u>, pp. 20-21.

(21)   <u>Ibid.</u>, p.20.

(22)   *Bill Braden Papers,* J.R. Doolittle, "A Motor Cycle Trip Across Europe", 1935.

(23)   <u>Ibid.</u>

In 1935, Mussolini's Italian Army, in its first foray beyond its own borders, attacked small and relatively defenseless Ethiopia, under the rule of Emperor Haile Selassie. Ethiopia soon fell beneath the Italian jackboot, and was added to their holdings in Africa. International tension arose over this blatant transgression, but despite Emperor Selassie appearing before the League of Nations to ask for help, the world stood by and let it happen in the hopes of preserving world peace. This policy of appeasing a dictator would continue right up to the outbreak of World War II.

(24)   <u>Ibid.</u>

(25)   <u>Ibid.</u>

(26)   <u>Ibid.</u>

(27)   <u>Ibid.</u>

(28)   <u>Ibid.</u>

(29)   *Bill Braden Papers,* Green Scrapbook.

(30)   Gwyn Buck letter to the author, 28 October 2009.

(31)   During World War II, 421 Squadron R.C.A.F. wrote to the company and got their permission to place McColl-Frontenac 's trademark symbol of an "Indian in a headdress" near the cockpit on each of their Spitfires. Ironically, one of the pilots in 421 Squadron was John McColl, the brother of Joan McColl.

(32)   *Bill Braden Papers,* Newspaper Clipping, @March 1939.

(33) *Bill Braden Papers*, Brown Photo Album 1941-1942.

(34) *Bill Braden Papers*, Brown Photo Album 1936-1939.

(35) <u>The Globe and Mail</u>, 4 December 1939, p. 12.

(36) "Braden-McColl", <u>Hamilton Spectator</u>, 4 December 1939.

(37) <u>Ibid.</u>

(38) It was located along the Third Concession at what was 345 Mountain Brow.

(39) John Braden to the author, Autumn 2009.

(40) *Library and Archives Canada Papers*, Lt.-Col. R. Neate O.C. #2 Det. R.C.O.C. to Officer Administering R.C.O.C., Ottawa, 7 January 1941.

Chapter 3-Endnotes

(1) Will's signing up with the Canadian Army would have been the topic of a good deal of discussion in the family, and would have been of the utmost interest to his stepfather-in-law. Since Francis Farwell's war effort consisted of being available to the Federal Government in an advisory capacity, as the Director of Mechanical Maintenance, he had no doubt made contact with those in the higher echelons of the Canadian Army, and felt that with those contacts, he could help facilitate his stepson-in-law's application for an officer's commission in the Army.

(2) *Library and Archives Canada Papers*, Lt. Col. R.Neate O.C. #2 Det. R.C.O.C. to Officer Administering, Royal Canadian Ordnance Corps, Ottawa, 7 January 1941.

(3) <u>Ibid.</u>, Lt.-Col. H.A. Campbell A.D.O.S. (A) to Officer Commanding No. 2 Detachment Royal Canadian Ordnance Corps (A.F.), Toronto, Ontario, 13 January 1941.

(4) <u>Ibid.</u>, Certificate of Medical Examination, 17 January 1941.

(5) <u>Ibid.</u>, Adjutant-General B.W. Browne to D.O.C. M.D. No. 2, Toronto, Ontario, 25 January 1941.

(6) <u>Ibid.</u>, Major-General C.F. Constantine D.O.C. M.D. No. 2 to The Secretary, Department of National Defence, Ottawa, Ontario, 18 February 1941.

(7) <u>Ibid.</u>, Record of Service of 2nd Lieut. William Greening Braden, n.d.

(8) <u>Ibid.</u>, Lt.-Col. H.A. Campbell A.D.O.S. (A) to Director of Personal Services, Department of National Defence, 6 March 1941.

(9)   Ibid., L.G. Francis to Director Personal Services, 14 May 1941.

(10) *Bill Braden Papers,* Personal Scrapbook.

(11) *Library and Archives Canada Papers,* op. cit., Brigadier G.C. Anglin D.O.C. M.D. No. 7 to the Secretary Department of National Defence, 27 June 1941.

(12) Ibid., Major W.W. Davis to O.A., R.C.O.C., 1 September 1941.

(13) Ibid., Telegram from Defensor to Canmilitary, 18 July 1941.

(14) Ibid., Colonel H.G. Thompson to D.O.S. (A), 24 September 1941.

(15) Ibid., Lt.-Col. C.L. Laurin to District Officers Commanding Military Districts No. 1 and No. 2, 1 October 1941.

(16) Ibid., Major K.H. McKibbin to D.O.S. (A), 13 October 1941.

(17) Ibid., Captain J.W.Collinge to Captain R.E. Slater, Paymaster No. 2 District Depot, Toronto, Ontario, 30 October 1941.

(18) Bill Braden Jr. interview with the author, Autumn 2009.

(19) *Library and Archives Canada Papers,* op. cit., Lieutenant-Colonel J.A.W. Bennett, A.Q.M.G. Canadian Military Headquarters to A.A.G. (M.S.) 19 November 1941.

(20) Ibid., Lieut.-Colonel J.A.W. Bennett, A.Q.M.G., C.M.H.Q. to M.S. (B), 28 February 1942.

(21) Ibid., Captain H.B. Mattson, O/C M.T. Inspectorate C.M.H.Q. to D.D.O.S. (E) C.M.H.Q., 29 April 1942.

(22) Ibid., Colonel H.B. Keenleyside, D.O.S. , Canadian Military Headquarters to A.A.G. (MS), 1 May 1942.

(23) *Bill Braden Papers*, Personal Photo Album.

(24) Ibid., Open letter from John Morley, n.d.

(25) Ibid., Open Letter from John Morley, March 1942.

(26) Ibid., "McNaughton Lays Cornerstone of New Base Ordnance Depot", April 1942.

(27) Ibid., "Hamiltonians Promoted Overseas", Hamilton Spectator, 16 June 1942.

(28) Ibid., Personal Photo Album

(29) Ibid.

(30) <u>Ibid.</u>

(31) <u>Ibid.</u>

(32) <u>Ibid.</u>

(33) <u>Ibid.</u>, "Bomb Wrecks Restaurant", <u>The Daily Mail</u>, 11 February 1943.

The attack was at tea time on 10 February. Accompanying the clipping, Braden has drawn on a sheet of paper, a floor plan of the school house, showing three windows for their offices, with his face in the far right window. Machine gun strikes were marked in red pencil. It was interesting to note that there were strikes both above and below the window in which Braden watched the attack unfold.

(34) Winston G. Ramsey ed., <u>The Blitz Then and Now-Volume 3</u>, London: Battle of Britain Prints International Limited, 1990, p. 216.

This was the period in the World War II air conflict where the German Luftwaffe was utilizing 'tip and run' tactics, where small groups of German bombers and fighters (Jabos) would sweep in over southern English towns close to the English Channel, and both bomb and machine gun the civilian populace. <u>The Blitz</u> book gave an overview of that February day's activities: "However on the 10th, 77 people were killed and 123 seriously injured in scattered attacks on Berkshire, Hampshire and Sussex, with Reading (41 killed), Newbury (19 fatalities), Midhurst and Chichester most affected…..Two Dornier 217's from 5/KG40 were shot down by anti-aircraft fire and crashed in England, with both crews of four airmen perishing….(pp. 216-219).

(35) *Bill Braden Papers*, W.G. Braden: Cars, Boats, Motorcycles File, R.A. Jensen to Bill Braden, 25 February 1943 and 28 April 1943.

(36) <u>Ibid.</u>, W.G. Braden: Cars, Boats and Motorcycles File, Anthony Brooke to Bill Braden, 10 March 1943.

(37) <u>Ibid.</u>, Personal Photo Album

(38) *Library and Archives Canada Papers*, Recommendation for William Greening Braden, 20 October 1943.

(39) <u>Ibid.</u>

(40) <u>Ibid.</u>, Brigadier H.B. Keenleyside TO AAG (MS), 2 March 1944.

(41) *Bill Braden Papers*, Personal Photo Album.

(42) Library *and Archives Canada Papers,* Brigadier J.H. MacQueen, D.Q.M.G. C.M.H.Q. to D.A.G. C.M.H.Q., 20 May 1944.

(43) *Bill Braden Papers,* 1944 Desk Diary.

Each day, Bill listed the people with whom he met/communicated; and the actions that he took. There was even time to note personal items, like Joan's birthday on 21 August, and the fact that he cabled her; and Billy's fourth birthday; or times that he ran into his brother in law, John McColl, or Basil Southam.

(44) *Library and Archives Canada* Papers, Major C.A. Mustard to Canadian Military Headquarters, 20 November 1944.

(45) Ibid., Colonel J.G. Pope, Canadian Military Headquarters Memorandum to DMGO (B), December 1944.

(46) bid., Major W.G. Braden to Major MacLaren, C.M.H.Q. 31 January 1945.

(47) Ibid., A.S. Ellis D.Q.M.G. Branch C.M.H.Q. to D.A.G. C.M.H.Q., 12 March 1945.

(48) Ibid., D.A.A.G. (L) to O.C. 1 Canadian Repatriation Depot, 15 March 1945.

(49) Ibid., Major-General A.E. Potts, D.O.C. M.D. No. 2 to The Secretary, Department of National Defence, Ottawa, Ontario, 24 April 1945.

(50) Ibid., Standard Recommendation Form-Officers, Canadian Army Active, 20 April 1945.

(51) Ibid., Request for Discharge, 1 August 1945.

(52) Ibid., Brigadier M. Noel to D.O.C. M.D. No. 2, 31 October 1945.

(53) Ibid., Medical Board Proceedings, 29 October 1945.

(54) Ibid. In his Desk Diary for 1944, Major Braden notes on both Friday 10 November, and Saturday 11 November "visited M.O. re knee."

(55) Ibid., Captain T. Goulding, Army Counsellor, Department of Veterans Affairs M.D. 12, 10 November 1945.

(56) Ibid.

(57) Ibid., Department of National Defence, Statement of War Service Gratuity, 9 January 1946.

(58) Ibid., Canadian Army (Active) Certificate of Service, Issued to Officers and Nursing Sisters, 19 December 1945.

(59) Norm Braden interview with the author, October 2009.

(60) *Bill Braden Papers,* Personal Scrapbook.

(61) Harcourt Bull interview with the author, October 2009.

<u>Chapter 4-Endnotes</u>

(1) *Bill Braden Papers,* op. cit., "Headed Transit Commission, Francis A. Farwell Dies At 72", <u>Hamilton Spectator</u>, @1966.

(2) *Bill Braden Papers,* Francis Farwell to Bill Braden, 19 July 1946.

(3) *Hamilton Street Railway Papers*, Box 66-Operational Files, File 8254, H.S.R. Personnel List, 7 January 1950.

(4) What gives us insights into Bill Braden's work career with the Company is the fact that the papers of Brigadier Stan Todd, the General Manager, to whom Bill Braden reported, are in the Company Archives. Braden was a member of the Management Co-Ordinating Committee, since he was a Department Head, and the Minutes of these 10 a.m. Monday meetings in Brigadier Todd's office explain the parameters of his job, and illustrate the duties he was asked to fulfill. The meetings were chaired by Brigadier Todd, and were run in a 'top down' fashion, where Mr. Todd directed the Department Heads to take action on problems that were brought up for discussion that pertained to their Department. The best description of the tenor of the meetings came from Brigadier Todd himself in the Minutes of 8 March 1955, when he "welcomed Mr. McColl...and briefly outlined the procedure followed at meetings. He stated that in transacting the business of the two companies [Canada Coach Limited and Hamilton Street Railway], the policy was set by Mr. Farwell with regard to both...and implemented by Mr. Todd, as General Manager with the assistance of Department Heads....Mr. Braden, with the title of Assistant General Manager, would have charge of the operating departments of the two companies....".

(5) *Hamilton Street Railway Papers*, Box 66-Operational Files, File 8419, Letters to Hamilton High School Principals 19 September 1950.

(6) <u>Ibid.</u>, Bill Braden to H.S. Alexander, 19 September 1950.

(7) <u>Ibid.</u>, File 8433, Bill Braden to Mrs. E. Corbett, 11 September 1950.

(8) <u>Ibid.</u>, Bill Braden to P.S.A. Todd, 19 September 1950

(9) Ibid., File 8416, Memo of Meeting of Bill Braden with Mr. Stipe (Hamilton Post Office), 11 May 1951.

The Hamilton Street Railway Company had a contract with the Post Office to provide four (4) free rides each weekday to each postman who was working.

(10) Ibid., Box 66-Operational Files, File 8575, Mrs. George Ritchie to Bill Braden, 4 June 1951.

(11) *Bill Braden Papers*, Francis Farwell to Bill Braden, 6 September 1951.

(12) *Hamilton Street Railway Papers*, Box 66-Operational Files, File 8419, Bill Braden to E.J.H. Ray, 19 September 1951.

This would include giving these groups access to either a 36 or 40 passenger bus at the same rate as a 27 passenger bus, which would be a discount of 30%.

(13) *Hamilton Street Railway Papers*, op.cit., File 8278, Minutes of Meeting of 14 January 1952

(14) Ibid. Minutes of Meeting of 3 March 1952.

(15) *Bill Braden Papers*, Hamilton Spectator, 24 April 1952.

(16) *Hamilton Street Railway Papers*, op.cit., Minutes of Meeting of 23 June 1952.

(17) Ibid., Minutes of Meeting of 30 June 1952.

The General Manager had in mind a set-up by which the two paint shops could be amalgamated to save the Company money.

(18) Ibid., Minutes of Meeting of 27 October 1952.

(19) Ibid., Minutes of Meeting of 3 November 1952.

In the early days of television, and considering the strength of the broadcast signal, the audio portion could be drowned out by the closer, stronger audio of the H.S.R. walkie-talkies.

(20) Ibid., Minutes of Meeting of 24 November 1952.

(21) Ibid., Minutes of Meetings of 1 & 8 December 1952.

(22) Ibid., Minutes of Meeting of 5 January 1953.

(23) Ibid., Minutes of Meeting of 12 January 1953.

(24) Ibid., Minutes of Meeting of 26 January 1953.

(25) <u>Ibid.</u>, Minutes of Meeting of 2 February 1953.

(26) <u>Ibid.</u>

(27) *Hamilton Street Railway Papers*, Box 67, File 8346, Memo from Bill Braden and J. Little to P.A.S. Todd, 6 February 1953.

(28) <u>Ibid.</u>, File 8278, Minutes of the Meeting of 9 February 1953.

(29) <u>Ibid.</u>, Minutes of the Meeting of 16 February 1953.

(30) <u>Ibid.</u>, Minutes of Meeting of 4 May 1953.

(31) <u>Ibid.</u>, Minutes of Meeting of 11 May 1953.

(32) <u>Ibid.</u>, Minutes of Meeting of 8 June 1953.

(33) <u>Ibid.</u>, Minutes of Meeting of 22 June 1953.

(34) <u>Ibid.</u>, Minutes of Meeting of 13 July 1953.

(35) <u>Ibid.</u>, Minutes of Meeting of 14 September 1953.

(36) <u>Ibid.</u>, Minutes of Meeting of 10 November 1953.

(37) <u>Ibid.</u>, Minutes of Meeting of 17 November 1953.

(38) <u>Ibid.</u>, Minutes of Meeting of 15 December 1953.

Other topics in 1953 included how Mr. Braden reported that for a six week period, Mountain buses would use James Street, Mountain Road, and Inverness to James Street, while Arkledun Avenue was closed to traffic (1 June 1953). Later in the month, Mr. Todd wanted Mr. Braden to talk about the proposed cancellation of service on non-paying routes (22 June 1953). Mr. Braden was to report on the plan for dealing with school certificates in the upcoming school term (24 July 1953). Mr. Braden was to make arrangements for a bus [turning] loop at one of the service stations located at the Mohawk Road and Gage Avenue intersection. Mr. Braden also reported that the new cruiser cars would be numbered 1152-1155 (10 October 1953). Mr. Braden was asked to negotiate for turnaround privileges [for buses] at the northeast corner of Gage and Mohawk at a monthly rental fee of $5 (24 November 1953). He was asked to present a recommendation about a decal to be placed on the new fare boxes asking passengers to deposit their own fares (21 December 1953).

(39) <u>Ibid.</u>, Minutes of Meeting of 5 January 1954.

(40) <u>Ibid.</u>, Minutes of Meeting of 10 March 1954.

(41) <u>Ibid.</u>, Minutes of Meeting of 16 March 1954.

(42) <u>Ibid.</u>, Minutes of Meeting of 10 August 1954.

(43) <u>Ibid.</u>, Minutes of Meeting of 20 October 1954.

(44) <u>Ibid.</u>, Minutes of Meeting of 10 November 1954.

Other topics in 1954 saw Mr. Braden noting Burlington route buses to continue through Burlington Street to Kenilworth Avenue on the outbound trip, and vice-versa on the return trip, thus eliminating the use of Gage Avenue and Beach Road, which would be an improvement in service. He also received a letter from Shell Oil Company requesting a letter absolving them from liability from possible accidents that might occur at their station at Gage and Mohawk when H.S.R. vehicles were looping on the property (5 January 1954). Mr. Todd requested that Mr. Braden make a tour that day regarding road conditions on the Mountain (16 February 1954). Mr. Todd requested that Mr. Braden keep a careful check of the situation at the Gore with the Bank of Nova Scotia ceremony that day, so that service might not be held up….Mr. Braden said that operators had been instructed to see that bus transfers were torn off properly. Mr. Braden disclosed that a map had been prepared of railway crossings, indicating unprepared areas (23 February 1954). Messrs Braden, Smith and Pickard were requested to check the mileage of White buses, which Mr. Todd said exceeded the budget by 800 miles in the past week. He emphasized that it was necessary for budget purposes to make certain that the Whites were not favored as against Brilles. Mr. Todd reminded Mr. Braden that he would like him and Mr. McCulloch to write down subject headings, discussing operator training, and when convenient, to write out the talk given for permanent record (23 March 1954). In connection with the arranging of turnaround facilities at Sunoco Oil Company's new service station at Parkdale and Beach Road, in lieu of the present situation involving the 'Harris' property, Mr. Braden said that details were being worked out by him (17 August 1954). Mr. Todd reminded Mr. Braden that he and others who lectured to operators were to submit a typewritten report of the substance of their talks by not later than November 16th, 1954. Mr. Todd asked Mr. Braden to keep a close check on track removal at Main and Sherman and King and Sherman and to go into the situation regarding restoration for direct service from the downtown area into Rosedale and to Parkdale (14 September 1954) Mr. Braden was asked to call Robinson Construction Company for a fixed date for roadwork to be done on Superior Street, and to learn the elapsed time before the railway would be operating on the street again (29 September 1954). Mr. Braden reported that he would make inquiries concerning the proposed blocking of Concession Street on Thanksgiving Day, between the hours of 9:30 a.m. and noon. If the police department have granted permission, Mr. Braden will arrange to detour the Jolley Cut buses over a suitable route during the above mentioned day and time (5 October 1954). Mr. Braden was to look into the Gage Avenue (Mountain) situation in order that the H.S.R. might be prepared to give one week's notice before again operating (12 October 1954). Mr. Todd stated that the GTA Convention held at Windsor on the 24th-26th November, would be attended by Mr. Braden, representing Mr. Todd who would not be present, and three other members of the Management Committee (3 November 1954). Mr. Braden was asked to go over the fuel oil, and lubricating and grease and gasoline tenders with Mr. Pickard and report their recommendations. Mr. Todd asked that Mr. Braden, on his return from Windsor, look into the matter of inspectors using cruising cars to pick up other supervisors coming to work, contrary to company rules (23 November 1954).

(45) Ibid., Minutes of the Meeting of 1 March 1955.

(46) Ibid., Minutes of the Meeting of 15 March 1955.

(47) Ibid., Minutes of the Meeting of 21 March 1955.

1955 Management Committee topics included that Mr. Braden could notify Canada Coach Lines, if he was satisfied that it was feasible, that sixteen H.S.R. buses, twelve 44's and four Brilles, would be available to them on loan, July 1st to September 1st for use at Niagara Falls, 'loan' being understood to mean rental (16 February 1955). Mr. Todd requested that Messrs Braden and Farebrother, consult as soon as possible, on operating procedures, in order that Mr. Braden might take over full responsibilities as Assistant General Manager in charge of Operating. Mr. Todd instructed that an information service be made by Messrs. Braden and Farebrother with regard to the possible reduction of schedules in Welland and Galt city operations (15 March 1955).

(48) Ibid., Minutes of the Meeting of 31 May 1955.

Other topics for the year included reducing the Sunday bus service in Galt from two buses to one bus (31 May 1955). Mr. Braden was asked to trace the reason why equipment ordered on Saturday night from Canada Coach Limited was late in arriving. Mr. Todd felt that the C.C.L. Dispatcher should advise Mr. Braden when he needed buses (20 June 1955). Mr. Todd asked Mr. Braden to check with the Operating Department to see that an accurate record was kept of H.S.R. buses called into service by C.C.L., including a notation of bus numbers. This was to keep mileage figures accurate. Mr. Braden was to check with Mr. Farebrother to find out if Steam Railway Company tickets and passes were to be honored on C.C.L. sightseeing vehicles (28 June 1955). It was decided to arrange for a luncheon to be attended by the Supervisors of both companies at the Wentworth Arms Hotel on Tuesday July 12th at 12:30. Recently initiated policy points were to be discussed (5 July 1955). Mr. Braden and a committee were to design a training program for C.C.L. drivers, with attention to weeks of training, rates of pay etc. Mr. Braden and a committee were to decide on a decorative scheme for new buses with regard to interiors (19 July 1955). Mr. Braden is to work out the details regarding the Operator Training Program (26 July 1955). In the absence of Mr. Braden until Tuesday August 9th, Mr. Farebrother would be responsible for equipment requirements, discipline etc. in the Operating Department (3 August 1955). On his return, Mr. Braden was to report regarding a letter to the editor of the Spectator re 'stops' (9 August 1955). Mr. Braden was to confer with two other members of the Management Committee regarding a new route on the Mountain to serve the new Collegiate Institute. Thought was to be given a suitable name for the route before transfers were ordered (16 August 1955). Mr. Braden was to see that new detour signs were posted on the Burlington Street route, informing the public of temporary detours in connection with the track removal program. Mr. Braden expressed concern over the wear and tear on the Burlington Street buses because of the condition of Beach Road, and running on Burlington Street as far as Kenilworth Avenue….Messrs Farebrother and Braden were requested to consult with regard to C.C.L. hiral requirements (30 August 1955). Mr. Braden said that Order #62 was being enforced making it obligatory for C.C.L. Operators on charter trips to remain by their equipment at all times (7 September 1955). Mr. Todd notified Mr. Braden that four of the H.S.R. Operators presently in C.C.L. service might be needed for a week or ten days more until the [summer] holidays are over (13 September 1955). Mr. Braden was to arrange for the return of the next group of H.S.R. buses from Niagara Falls, after the weekend (23 September 1955). Mr. Braden reported that ten men had been selected from the spare board to operate the Dundas service, and operators presently on Dundas would take over the Burlington run (1 November 1955). Mr. Braden was to design a suitable paint scheme in consultation with the foreman painter, for the interior and exterior of the new vehicles, four GM coaches of the 1700 series, and to submit his recommendation by the next meeting. Messrs Pickard and Braden were to supply Mr. Todd with a list of the 400 series with the description as to side doors, fare boxes etc. Mr. Braden said that H.S.R. interurban trainees were to be given instruction in gear changing on the 1600 coaches (8 November 1955). Mr. Braden was to see that cards at bus stops on the San and Ancaster route be removed four or five days after the changeover takes place on Wednesday. Mr. McCulloch felt that something should be done to eliminate delays on the bus terminal switchboard, and Messrs McColl, Braden, and Farebrother were appointed to act as a committee to investigate the situation, and to report back on their findings within a couple of weeks (15 November 1955). Mr. Todd asked both Mr. Braden and Mr. Pickard to check the fare box collection system to see that a rotating schedule was being maintained. Mr. Braden said that all temporary cardboard signs placed at bus stops on the Burlington,

Dundas, and Sanitorium routes have been removed (22 November 1955). Mr. Braden stated that he was preparing a script to be followed by operators at the bus terminal when using the public address system (27 November 1955). Mr. Braden and Mr. McColl were to go over the list of those to be invited to the C.C.L. Supervisory group luncheon at the Wentworth Arms, Thursday December 20th….Messrs Braden and Smith were to confer on Dofasco's request for rental of ten large buses on December 24th. Mr. Braden and Mr. Little were to check with Mr. Barnes as to possible irregularities in ticket sales by operators on the Dundas route….Mr. Braden asked for a report from the Accounting Department comparing business being done on the interurban routes with last year's business (6 December 1955). Mr. Braden said that the script for departure announcements had been finished (13 December 1955). Mr. Braden was asked to report why it was that a bus due out of the terminal at 9 a.m. had been seen by Mr. Todd at Main and James at 8:57 a.m. (20 December 1955). Mr. Braden reported that the training of men on the new routes was well in hand….The meeting confirmed that time and a quarter was the proper basis for pay on Sunday December 25th, and time and a half for Monday December 26th. Mr. Braden was to get in touch with Mr. White (Niagara Falls) to this effect….(27 December 1955).

(49) Ibid., Minutes of the Meeting of 25 January 1956.

Other topics discussed that spring included: Mr. Todd asked Mr. Braden to have a check made by the supervisors for one day on transfers. He said that he was aware that some operators were punching up hours in advance of time, and he wished this to be stopped….Messrs Braden, Smith and Pickard were asked to present recommendations regarding Pottriff Road service whereby changeovers might be held ready in the area during certain hours of the operating day to eliminate lengthy delays in service if the bus line broke down….(25 January 1956). The concluding part of the meeting was devoted to a discussion of the Operating Establishment, with Mr. Braden expressing the opinion that it should be decided without delay how many men were needed by the H.S.R. in order that hiring should be done if necessary (7 February 1956). Mr. Braden was to issue an order that interurban operators were to cash in at the terminal after Mr. Little had set the date (14 February 1956).

(50) *Hamilton Street Railway Papers*, Box 63, File 8343, Statement of Policy-Operators, Memo from P.A.S. Todd, 12 March 1956.

(51) Ibid., File 8278, Minutes of the Meeting of 13 March 1956.

There were other discussions that merit note. Mr. Farebrother said that there would have to be a replacement for Mr. Oliver in the Ticket Office, who was ill in the hospital. Mr. Todd asked Mr. Braden and Mr. Farebrother to deal with the matter….Mr. Braden, discussing the Wilbur-Smith plan for one way streets felt that Gore Street should be left as a two way thoroughfare for at least three blocks to facilitate the movement of vehicles out of the bus terminal….Mr. Todd said that Mr. Braden should instruct Mr. White to have operators of buses serving boat passengers to telephone in to learn their reporting time at the dock….The meeting also indicated its approval of Mr. Braden's recommendation that Mr. Farebrother proceed to apply to the proper authorities to operate the Milton bus on the Guelph Line instead of Appleby Road….Mr. Braden was critical of the use of Brills on the Aberdeen and York routes on Sunday, and it was agreed that there should be a check made as to the difference in the cost of operating Brills and Fords (13 March 1956). Mr. Braden reported that the Fort Erie race service was working very well (17 April 1956). Messrs Braden and Farebrother were to attend the meetings of the Ontario Association of Motor Coach Operators May 16th and 17th. Mr. Todd asked Mr. Braden and Mr. Farebrother to bring in their recommendations on revised charter rates at the next meeting (1 May 1956). Dr. Tice would in the future, do all yearly medical check-ups of C.C.L. operators. Mr. Braden was instructed to notify department heads at outside divisions, of this policy….Mr. Todd cautioned Mr. Braden to be sure that summer drivers received sufficient training before putting them to work (5 June 1956) . Because of the continual and rapid expansion of areas within the city, which were removed by more than normal distance from the Company's established groups, Mr. Todd felt that Mr. Braden and himself should make a tour of the city as soon as possible to consider the various changes in routing to meet the present and future need (12 June 1956). Mr. Braden was asked to notify Mr. White that he must see that regular Operators were not to do sightseeing work, while summer men with little or no experience were placed on regular runs. Mr. Todd said that one of the latter drivers had been 40 minutes late the previous Sunday….The meeting dealt with points arising out of the Wilbur Smith report, applying to one way streets. Mr. Smith was also to turn over to Mr. Braden a typewritten list of routes and other pertinent information. Mr. Todd asked Mr. Braden to commence work on lining up the entire proposition to have everything in readiness before going to the Committee….Mr. Todd set up a Committee on uniforms (both Companies) composed of the following: Mr. Braden [as] Chairman, and three others. There was a trend towards similar types of uniform and practices governing issues of the same, but he wishes the Committee to examine the situation thoroughly before reporting its findings (19 June 1956). Mr. Braden was asked to have the Committee on uniforms make recommendations as to future policy (26 June 1956). Mr. Todd said that the one way street system in Hamilton would become effective Sunday October 28th…. Mr. Braden was asked to have H.S.R. and C.C.L. 'stops' changed in time to make application to the Traffic Committee on October 1st (11 September 1956)

(52) File 8333, Management Control Chart, Bill Braden & John McColl to P.A.S. Todd, May 1956.

(53) Ibid., Francis Farwell to Bill Braden, 11 May 1956.

[As you read the letter, you can feel the rap across the knuckles from Mr. Farwell]

(54) Box 66, File 8278, Minutes of H.S.R. Management Co-Ordinating Committee, Minutes of Meeting of 25 September 1956.

Other topics covered late in the year included: Mr. Braden and Mr. Pickard were to work out, if possible, a satisfactory solution to providing Mr. White at Niagara Falls , with two 1700s for a charter booking to the U.S.(25 September 1956). Mr. Braden would attend to the matter of signs reading 'power on' and 'power off' for the King-Barton and Cannon Operators direction at Hughson and King Streets....Mr. Todd asked Mr. Braden to see that power was pulled at @8:45 p.m. on the K-B and Cannon trolley routes on Saturday October 27th in order that switches might be cut in for the one way street programme which would go into effect the following day. Trolleys would be taken off service and Whites substituted for them. The same would apply on Sunday morning. It was expected that at least 12 hours would be required for the changeover (2 October 1956). Mr. Braden also was to clear with the operators with regard to the coming weekend change, and to have an inspector at King and James Street to make sure that operators continued through to Main Street rather than turning east at Birks....Mr. Braden was requested to contact Mr. Lomax about marking off Main Street East this weekend and if possible to try to have the curbs painted at downtown points prior to the 28th (9 October 1956). Mr.Todd asked Mr. Braden to see that operators call out to persons waiting at what were former bus stops, to advise them where their new stop was located (16 October 1956). Mr. Todd stated that officials in charge of the Remembrance Day ceremonies had written in complimentary terms about the H.S.R. arrangements made by Mr. Braden....Messrs. Braden and McCulloch were requested to keep the afternoon and evening of Monday November 19th open, since they were to be the guests of the City, along with others who had helped in the planning and introduction of one way streets....Mr. Todd authorized Messrs. Braden and Smith to spend up to a thousand dollars for additional supervisors and checkers to report on the actions of Operators as well as private citizens [regarding trucks and cars parked at bus stops and doing double parking](13 November 1956). Mr. Todd asked Mr. Braden to deal with Mr. Lomax...and to request that the bus areas be clearly painted since the situation could not continue (20 November 1956). Mr. Todd further said he wanted to have a conference with Messrs. Braden [and 3 other Committee members] with regard to buses to see if the C.C.L. fleet could be reduced in number.... Mr. Braden said Mr. Spalding, Hamilton Board of Education, had inquired as to the cost daily of two buses to transport Beach children to Saltfleet school (27 November 1956). Mr. Braden and Mr. Smith were to meet that afternoon at 2:00 o'clock with Mr. Lomax and Assistant Police Chief Moreau regarding double parking (4 December 1956)....it was agreed that Mr. Farebrother in the future would send a copy of the Interurban Bulletin to Mr. Braden who would have a copy for suburban operators typed by Miss Holowich and posted....Mr. Braden said that a standardized script had been printed and would be posted. This had to do with drivers announcements over the speakers. Mr. Braden was to issue an order that, in cases when bus departures were held up for connections, the driver of the bus delayed was to notify his passengers as to the reason....Mr. Braden would see L.T. Spalding, Board of Education about Beach school bus service to Saltfleet....Mr. Todd requested Mr. Braden to go into the matter of Express buses within the City, and to report back on his findings (17 December 1956).

(55)   Box 67, File 8333-Management Control Chart, Bill Braden to all Department Heads, 27 August 1957.

(56)   Ibid., P.A.S. Todd to Managers, 11 December 1957.

(57)   Box 68, File 8287-Purchase of Sarnia Transit, G.A.M. Thomas to P.A.S. Todd, 22 July 1958.

(58)   Ibid., P.A.S. Todd to the Mayor of Sarnia, 1 August 1958.

(59)   Ibid., P.A.S. Todd to the Mayor of Sarnia, 11 August 1958.

(60)   Ibid., Memo by Bill Braden re the Sarnia Transit Company Limited, 18 August 1958.

Included with those generalities were 1 ½ pages of specific responsibilities that had to be accomplished before the inauguration of the bus service in Sarnia.

This marks the end of the written documentation of Bill Braden's work as Assistant General Manager (Operations) at both the Hamilton Street Railway and the Canada Coach Lines. The fact that any of these materials have survived to the benefit of the historian is due to the tireless work of Cindy Slinn, presently Marketing Co-Coordinator, in the Transit Division of the Public Works Department of the City of Hamilton. Her story of the creation of the Hamilton Street Railway Archives illustrates the fine line between preservation and loss of historical documents:

"The Wentworth Street Garage...opened on August 26, 1926. All employees (except for the Planning staff....)worked out of that location until 1984. In 1984, the Mountain Garage was built and Mountain route buses were relocated to this facility along with some staff....We continued to use 18 Wentworth Street Garage for downtown routes and some administrative staff.

Once the building at 330 Wentworth Street was completed in 1990, all equipment and staff were moved to this location. 18 Wentworth Street was demolished and 2200 Upper James was rented out as office space.

I started in 1989 at the Mountain location. At that time, there was not a formal Archive room, but we did have boxes of files, photos and 'stuff' that started accumulating when the Mountain garage was built and people started to move around. That collection landed in the Marketing and Customer Service area. I am sure each section had their own little stash of interesting memorabilia and files, but it wasn't really shared with others. There was a storage office upstairs at 18 Wentworth Street that contained items when people retired or office cleanups were done. It was not organized and most boxes were covered in a layer of dust when it came time to move….After the staff moved out of 18 Wentworth Street during 1989/1990, Carole Morris-McHugh (Communications Officer) and myself (Customer Service Representative) went to the old facility to take photos before it was destroyed. There were interesting things left behind that staff didn't know what to do with. We found old files, interesting artifacts, old fixtures etc., and collected what we could. We then spread the word to employees that we would take archives. Things started to accumulate at that point. A number of photos, newspaper clippings, files, uniforms and old office equipment started coming our way by employees. Our employees knew they shouldn't throw it out, but didn't know what to do with it. The formal archive room was then established at 330 Wentworth Street North. I still have things coming to me to put in the archive room as people retire or clean out files etc.

…there was no real plan to collect these items. Most items had been collected and stored in Marketing & Customer Services at this time, but some boxes and equipment had been left in the building. When the storage area at 18 Wentworth St. N. was emptied, it fell into the Marketing & Customer Service area. Our Supervisor. John Gosgnach, Carole and myself understood the importance of keeping these items together and tried to collect as much as we could before things were destroyed. We didn't really know what we had until we started going through the boxes and tried to organize them….As you know, I find these items very interesting, entertaining and I realize we must preserve our heritage/history. Somehow, unofficially, the Archives have stayed with me to maintain. HSR was always seen as a separate entity from the City. That is why the history of the HSR doesn't really exist with the City, they came in late in the process and didn't really recognize us until a decade or so ago. I am sure a great deal of articles/items went with the previous owners when the HSR changed hands…." (Cindy Slinn to the author, 16 April 2010).

(61)   Interview with the author 5 May 2010,

(62) *Bill Braden Papers*, Scrapbook, 1947.

Ironically, as Bill Braden Jr. noted to the author, there was no Waterdown motorcycle club. His dad would just come and start riding in the races.

(63) *Bill Braden Papers*, H.R. Taylor to Bill Braden, 3 February 1948.

(64) *Bill Braden Papers*, <u>The Boar</u>, #19, January 1952, p. 59.

(65) *Bill Braden Papers*, <u>The Boar</u>, #20, January 1953, p. 20

(66) *Bill Braden Papers*, <u>The Boar</u>, #21, February 1954, pp. 44-45

(67) Bill Braden Jr. interview with the author, Autumn 2009.

(68) Bill Braden Jr. interview with the author, 2009.

Both Bill Braden Jr. and the author are in agreement that what his Dad was trying to do with the 1957 trip was to recreate his 1935 European motorcycle trip and to take his wife and sons to all the places he had travelled. As well, it was imperative that a Canadian boater meet the Duke of York organizers to present a positive image to get their approval for the race to be held in Canada and outside Great Britain.

(69) Bill Braden Jr. interview with the author, 2009.

Chapter 5-Endnotes

(1) *Bill Braden Papers,* Brown Photo Album 1941-42.

(2) *Bill Braden Papers*, Norman Braden to Will Braden, 18 July 1940.

(3) *Bill Braden Papers*, Norman Braden to Will Braden, 24 July 1940.

(4) *Bill Braden Papers*, <u>New York Times</u>, 20 July 1947.

(5) *Bill Braden Papers*. "Canadian Wins Feature Boat Race", 1946.

Braden's **Ariel II** was a 1939 eighteen foot Ventnor racing hull. Since 1902, the Ventnor Boat Corporation of Atlantic, New Jersey, had gained fame as builders of the world's fastest speed boats. Before World War II, with advanced designs and a group of highly skilled workers, the plant concentrated on turning out custom built racing boats for individuals primarily interested in winning races and establishing new records. Famous Ventnor-made boats included **Miss Peps V** and **Tempo VI.**

During World War II, the company built 83' and 104' aircraft rescue boats for the Army, and 110' sub chasers for the Navy. They received the 'Army-Navy E Award' for excellence of construction and outstanding performance. [In postwar America] It was confidently expected that their new Gold Cup boats, with the great power now available [with aircraft engines], would be able to reach and surpass the world's [speed] record of 141.74 m.p.h. held at the time by [Sir Malcolm] Campbell. See "Ventnor-Speed Merchants", Motor Boating, October 1947, pp. 99-100.

Ariel II was classified as a 225 cubic inch class hydroplane, powered by a Lycoming six cylinder, 175 h.p. engine, which turned the bronze prop at 5,000 r.p.m. The boat had had a variety of owners and names before it came to Braden. In 1939, it raced as 'Apache II' and was owned by Robert Joite from Joite, Ohio. That year it was the winner of the Picton Gold Cup 225 Division I class. In 1940 it was owned by David G. Sorensen of Buffalo, New York, and raced as 'Englett III'. She repeated as the winner at Picton, and won as well at the Quebec Championship 225 Division I at Valleyfield, Quebec, with a speed of 63.7 m.p.h. She attained a sixth place at Red Bank, New Jersey, in the same 225 class, and ended second in the Canadian championships in Toronto for her class. In 1941, Albert Brinkman from Buffalo, New York took over the boat, and changed her name to 'Seabiscuit'. The boat finished in second place, and won the B.A. High Point Trophy for her Division in Canada. With the war, the boat did not race again until Braden purchased the hull in 1946.

During his racing career, Bill Braden entered boats in the following three classes:

135 cubic inch class boats had a total maximum piston displacement that did not exceed 135 cubic inches. Competing boats were to be empowered by one internal combustion motor of the four cycle type. The cost of the power plant was not to exceed $1000. Fuel was to be restricted to methanol only. The minimum length of the boat was to be 13 feet 6 inches. The boat's number was to be preceded by the letter 'A'. A race for this class of boat was not less than two heats of five miles in length.

The 225 cubic inch class was designated and promoted for the purpose of establishing a class of inboard racing boats, the cost of which would be low enough to attract the average racing enthusiast. It was open to any boat powered with a stock automobile motor not exceeding 226 cubic inches in displacement. The cost of the motor and all extras as finished products was not to exceed $600. Fuel was restricted to gasoline of a rating not higher than 100 octane. Blends of gasoline and alcohol were prohibited. The minimum length of the boat was to be 16 feet. The letter prefix for this class of boats was 'N'.

The 266 cubic inch class was to have a maximum piston displacement of not in excess of 266 cubic inches. Competing boats were to be powered by one or more internal combustion motors of the four cycle non supercharged type. A completely installed power plant was to cost no more than $1250. Fuel usage was restricted to methanol only. The boat must carry a racing number preceded by the letter 'F'. The race was to consist of not less than two heats of five miles in length.

(6)   *Bill Braden Papers*, "Hamiltonians Make Mark In Powerboat Contests", Hamilton Spectator, 19 July 1947.

(7)   *Bill Braden Papers,* Ivan Miller, "The Sports Trail", Hamilton Spectator, 31 August 1946, p. 24.

(8)   *Bill Braden Papers*, Frank Kenesson, "Lombardo Sets Record in Winning Gold Cup", Globe and Mail, 3 September 1946.

(9)   *Bill Braden Papers*, "Hamiltonians Make Mark In Powerboat Contests", op. cit.

(10) *Bill Braden Papers*, "Brooklyn Driver Takes Speedboat Title at Belleville".

(11) *Bill Braden Papers*, Harry Leduc, "Surface Smooth" The Detroit News, 13 July 1947.

In winning the Detroit race, Braden surpassed Bob Bogie, who was the top Division 1, 225 class driver in the late 1940s. A native of Brooklyn, New York, Bogie had been with the U.S. Fifteenth Air Force, operating out of Italy. When his bomber crashed, he was seriously burned, and it took twelve different surgeries to ensure his survival.

(12) *Bill Braden Papers*, Tommy Devine, "Ford Cup Race", Detroit Free Press, 13 July 1947.

(13) *Bill Braden Papers*, "Hamiltonians Make Mark in Powerboat Contests", op.cit.

(14) *Bill Braden Papers,* Harry Leduc, "Miss Canada III 200 Yards Back", Detroit News, 31 August 1947.

(15) *Bill Braden Papers*, "Notre Dame Captures O.J. Mulford Silver Cup", Motor Boating, October 1947, pp. 98-99.

(16) *Bill Braden Papers*, "70 Year Old Veteran Race Star", The Hamilton Spectator, 3 August 1948.

(17) *Bill Braden Papers*, "Beloved 'Pops' Cooper Drove To His Death", Picton's Mainsail, 1 August 1949.

(18) *Bill Braden Papers*, George Carver, "Belleville Sports Writer Gives Regatta Impressions", Picton's Mainsail, 1 August 1949.

(19) *Bill Braden Papers*, Harry Leduc, "She Takes First Heat", Detroit News, 5 September 1948.

(20) *Bill Braden Papers,* <u>The Flint Journal</u>, 5 September 1948.

(21) *Bill Braden Papers,* "Speedboat Explodes At Bayfront, Owner Suffers Burns", <u>Hamilton Spectator</u>, Monday 22 August 1949.

(22) *Bill Braden Papers*, "Street Features Speedboat Races With Two Firsts", <u>Globe and Mail</u>, 14 July 1949.

(23) *Bill Braden Papers*, "Buffalo Boat Driver Skims Over Picton Bay at 45.825 Miles an Hour", <u>Globe and Mail</u>, 2 August 1949.

(24) *Bill Braden Papers*, <u>Boating Magazine</u>, October 1949, p. 23.

(25) *Bill Braden Papers*, "Lombardo Wins, Loses In Boat Races at CNE", <u>Globe and Mail</u>, 6 September 1953.

(26) *Bill Braden Papers*, Denny Harvey, "Hamilton Enthusiasts Building Powerboat Prestige", <u>Hamilton Spectator</u>, 18 March 1950.

(27) *Bill Braden Papers,* Dennis Harvey, "High Spots Are High For 100 m.p.h.", <u>Hamilton Spectator</u>, 25 July 1951.

<u>Hot Rod Magazine </u>did an article in January 1952, noting that **Alter Ego** (F-1) was the only boat in the world powered by a converted passenger car engine, a 266 cubic inch Flat Head Ford Mercury. In 1950 at Salton Sea, California, [an inland sea some 250 feet below sea level in the California desert] it set a two way average speed of 115 m.p.h., and on one of those runs, attained a speed of 117 m.p.h. It raised the previous speed record by 15 m.p.h. It was referred to by <u>Speed and Spray </u>magazine as 'The World's Fastest Limited Hydroplane'. In November 1951, they went back to Salton Sea, and raised the bar higher, obtaining a two way mile speed of 120.083 m.p.h. This marked the first time in boating history that **any boat** in the 225 class topped the 120 m.p.h. speed mark.

(28) Bill Braden Jr. interview with the author, 18 February 2010.

(29) Bill Braden Jr interview with the author, Autumn 2009.

(30) *Bill Braden Papers*, "Daoust Boat First In Quebec Regatta", <u>New York Times</u>, 22 July 1951.

(31) *Bill Braden Papers*, "Daoust Sweeps Hydroplane Race at Valleyfield", <u>Globe and Mail</u>, 23 July 1951.

(32) *Bill Braden Papers*, Bob Finlayson, "Braden Breaks 100 mph", <u>Boating Magazine</u>, September 1951, p. 21.

(33) *Bill Braden Papers*, "Cooking With Gas", <u>Hamilton News</u>, 23 July 1951.

(34) *Bill Braden Papers*, "Braden Hits 90 To Score Early", <u>Hamilton Spectator</u>, 30 July 1951.

(35) *Bill Braden Papers*, Bob Finlayson, "Braden Breaks 100 mph", <u>Boating Magazine</u>, <u>op. cit.</u>, p. 26.

(36) *Bill Braden Papers*, "Brayden Takes Event Plaudits But Langmuir Takes Gold Cup", <u>The Picton Times</u>, 9 August 1951.

(37) *Bill Braden Papers*, "Regatta Notes", <u>The Picton Times</u>, 9 August 1951.

(38) *Bill Braden Papers*, Bob Finlayson, "Braden Breaks 100 mph", <u>Boating Magazine</u>, <u>op. cit.</u>, p. 20

(39) *Bill Braden Papers*, <u>Boating Magazine</u>, September 1951, p. 31.

(40) *Bill Braden Papers*, "The 'Winner' Timed by Bulova", <u>Boating Magazine</u>, 1951.

(41) *Bill Braden Papers*, 'Canadian and International Utility-Inboard-Outboard Motor Boat Championships' Brochure-1951.

(42) *Bill Braden Papers*, "Bill Braden Wins Award", <u>Hamilton Spectator</u>, 7 September 1951.

(43) *Bill Braden Papers*, "An Indignity Indeed", <u>Globe and Mail</u>, 4 August 1952, p.1.

(44) *Bill Braden Papers*," Braden's Boat Sinks After Race Accident", <u>Hamilton Spectator</u>, 5 August 1952.

(45) *Bill Braden Papers*, Detroit newspaper, n.d.

(46) *Bill Braden Papers*," Speed and More Speed at the Waterfront Saturday", <u>Globe and Mail</u>, 5 August 1953.

(47) *Bill Braden Papers*, "Escapade I Is Winner of Nickel Cup Event", <u>Globe and Mail</u>, 2 July 1954.

(48) Braden himself was unsure as to what his final position was. He wrote in his scrapbook 'sixth or seventh'.

Chapter 6-Endnotes

(1) *Jim Thompson Papers*, "Miss Supertest 1951" File, Jim Thompson to Hiram K. Smith [True Magazine], 9 December 1951.

(2) <u>Ibid</u>., F.J. Moore to Jim Thompson, 4 June 1951.

When asked by the author in October 2009 about how Bill Braden came to be the first Supertest driver, Jim Thompson said that it was because of Harry Greening. He said that his dad was a good friend of Mr. Greening, who obviously would have recommended his nephew when asked on the issue by Colonel Thompson.

(3) *Bill Braden Papers*, "Capsule Comment", <u>Globe and Mail</u>, 23 August 1951.

(4) *Bill Braden Papers,* "Bill Braden May Drive Famed Boat", <u>Hamilton Spectator</u>, 30 August 1951.

(5) *Bill Braden Papers*, "To Enter Miss Supertest in President's Cup Race", <u>Hamilton Spectator</u>, 8 September 1951.

(6) *Jim Thompson Papers*, "W.G. Braden 1951-1957" File, Gordon Thompson to Bill Braden, 2 July 1952.

(7) *Jim Thompson Papers*, "Races 1952" File, H.B. Rutherford to Jim Thompson, 30 June 1952.

(8) *Jim Thompson Papers*, "W.G. Braden 1951-1957" File, Gordon Thompson to Bill Braden, 3 September 1952.

(9) Interview with Jim Thompson.

(10) *Jim Thompson Papers*, "Races 1953" File, Jim Thompson to Bill Braden, 9 September 1953.

(11) *Jim Thompson Papers*, "3 Pointer, Staudacher etc" File, Gordon Thompson to Harry Greening, 18 December 1953.

(12) The ruling was that the boat's hull and engine had to be constructed in the entrant's home country. So with the boat being built in Sarnia, and the engine coming from England (with Canada being a member of the British Commonwealth of Nations), the Thompsons were within the legal bounds to make a challenge for the Harmsworth Trophy.

(13) *Jim Thompson Papers*, "Messrs. Hall and Turner" File, Jim Thompson to Jim Hall, 8 September 1954.

(14) *Jim Thompson Papers*, Gordon Thompson Memo "Miss Supertest II", 31 October 1954.

(15) *Bill Braden Papers*, "Bill Braden Will Drive In Top Speedboat Tests", <u>Hamilton Spectator</u>, 14 June 1955.

(16) *Jim Thompson Papers*, Harry Eisen, "Miss Supertest Cracks Two Records In Race", <u>The London Free Press</u>, 20 June 1955.

(17) *Jim Thompson Papers*, Harry Eisen, "The Sports Picture", <u>The London Free Press</u>, 21 June 1955, p.23.

(18) *Jim Thompson Papers,* "Miss Supertest-H.B. Greening" File, Gordon Thompson to Harry Greening, 20 June 1955.

(19) *Jim Thompson Papers*, Harry Eisen, "Supertest Struck, Forced From Race", <u>The London Free Press</u>, 25 June 1955.

(20) *Jim Thompson Papers*, Ivan Miller, "The Sport Trail", <u>The Hamilton Spectator</u>, 28 June 1955.

(21) *Jim Thompson Papers*, Harry Eisen, "The Sports Picture", <u>The London Free Press</u>, 28 June 1955.

(22) *Jim Thompson Papers*, "St. Clair Regatta" Memo, Gordon Thompson to Jim Thompson, 17 July 1955.

(23) *Bill Braden Papers*, "1955 Gold Cup Race Lap By Lap", <u>Seattle Post-Intelligencer</u>, 8 August 1955, p. S17.

(24) *Bill Braden Papers*, Don Hunt, "Miss Supertest Damaged Setting Canadian Record", <u>Toronto Telegram</u>, 1 November 1955.

(25) *Jim Thompson Papers*, "Harmsworth 1956" File, Commodore R.B. Finlayson to Leonard Thompson, 27 December 1955.

(26) *Jim Thompson Papers*, Ted Douglas, "Final Test Run for Speedy Craft", <u>The Windsor Daily Star</u>, 20 June 1956.

(27) *Jim Thompson Papers,* Harry Eisen, "U.S. Craft Wins Maple Leaf Regatta, Miss Supertest Third", <u>The London Free Press</u>, 25 June 1956.

(28) *Jim Thompson Papers*, Gordon Thompson "Confidential" Memo, 24 June 1956.

(29) *Jim Thompson Papers*, Harry Eisen, "**Miss Supertest II** An Easy Winner in Picton Unlimited Class Races", <u>The London Free Press</u>, 2 July 1956.

(30) *Bill Braden Papers,* Jim Hunt, "Can **Miss Supertest II** Take the Harmsworth?", <u>Toronto Star</u>, 11 August 1956.

(31) Colonel Schleeh interview with the author, August 1998.

(32) *Jim Thompson Papers*, Harry Eisen, "London Boat Wallows Behind speedy **Shanty**, Needs 'Miracle' To Win", <u>The London Free Press</u>, 27 August 1956.

(33) *Jim Thompson Papers*, Matt Dennis, "Spinnin on Sport", <u>The Windsor Daily Star</u>, 27 August 1956.

(34) *Jim Thompson Papers,* Harry Leduc, "Why Canadian Boat Is Disappointment", <u>The Detroit News</u>, 27 August 1956.

(35) *Jim Thompson Papers,* Tommy Devine, "Some Hasty Changes In Order For Supertest", <u>The Detroit Free Press</u>, 27 August 1956.

(36) *Jim Thompson Papers*, Harry Leduc, "Why Canadian Boat Is Disappointment", <u>op.cit.</u>

(37) <u>Ibid.</u>

(38) *Jim Thompson Papers*, Harry Eisen, "London Boat Wallows Behind Speedy **Shanty**, Needs 'Miracle' To Win", <u>op.cit.</u>

(39) *Jim Thompson Papers*, George Van, "**Miss Supertest** Wins As **Shanty**'s Motors Go Dead", <u>The Detroit Times</u>, 28 August 1956.

(40) Colonel Schleeh interview with the author, August 1998.

(41) *Bill Braden Papers,* Harry Leduc, "Defeated Driver Overcome in Boat", <u>The Detroit News</u>, 29 August 1956.

(42) *Jim Thompson Papers*, "Miscellaneous-Miss Supertest 1957" File, Dr. Aage Neilsen M.D. to H.B. Rutherford, 5 September 1956.

(43) <u>Ibid.</u>, Gordon Thompson to Donald Guerin, 20 August 1957.

(44) *Jim Thompson Papers*, Matt Dennis, "**Shanty I** Retains Harmsworth Trophy for U.S.", <u>The Windsor Daily Star</u>, 29 August 1956, p. 26.

(45) *Jim Thompson Papers*, "Miss Supertest-H.B. Greening" File, Gordon Thompson to Harry Greening, August 1956.

(46) *Jim Thompson Papers,* "Jones Would Help Canada", <u>The Windsor Daily Star</u>, 29 August 1956, p. 25.

(47) *Jim Thompson Papers*, George Van, "Canadian Driver Proves Champ Losing Harmsworth", <u>The Detroit Times</u>, 29 August 1956.

(48) Russ Schleeh to the author, August 1998, <u>op.cit.</u>

Chapter 7-Endnotes

(1) *Bill Braden Papers,* Al Nickleson, "Power boaters Will Vie for Expensive Trophy", <u>Globe and Mail</u>, 14 January 1958, p. 3.

(2) *Bill Braden Papers*, Bob Finlayson, "Canadians Triumph Abroad", <u>Boating Magazine</u>, Volume 26, Number 12, December 1951, pp.16-17.

(3) *Bill Braden Papers,* Audio Interview of Bill Braden by Art Asbury, Summer 1958.

(4) *Bill Braden Papers*, Bob Finlayson, "Duke of York Trophy Tragedy", <u>Boating Magazine</u>, n.d., p. 16

(5) <u>Ibid</u>.

(6) *Bill Braden Papers*, "Asbury Dares Death, Dives from **Miss Muskoka** to Find Pilot Killed in Collision", <u>Huntsville Forester</u>, n.d.

(7) *Bill Braden Papers*, "Death of Famed Canadian Driver in Fairy Lake Hydroplane Crash Cancels Big Speed-Boat Classic", n.d.

(8) *Bill Braden Papers*, "Canadian Boat Ace Killed by a Propeller in Huntsville Race", <u>Globe and Mail</u>, 1 September 1958.

(9) *Bill Braden Papers*, Bill Brennan, "Powerboat Survivor Ponders Retirement", <u>Detroit Free Press</u>, n.d.

(10) *Bill Braden Papers*, "Bill Braden's Widow Will Receive Trophy, Leaves Six Children", n.d.

(11) *Bill Braden Papers,* Harry Eisen, "Bill Braden's Death Shocks Many Here", <u>London Free Press</u>, 2 September 1958.

(12) *Bill Braden Papers*, Ivan Miller, "The Sport Trail", <u>Hamilton Spectator</u>, n.d.

(13) *Bill Braden Papers,* "Editorial", <u>Hamilton Spectator</u>, 2 September 1958.

(14) *Bill Braden Papers*, "Sportsman, HSR Executive Bill Braden Dies in Crash", <u>Hamilton Spectator</u>, 2 September 1958.

(15) *Bill Braden Papers*, George Van, "Bill Couldn't Stay Away', n.d.

(16) <u>Trinity College School Record</u>, December 1958.

(17) *Bill Braden Papers*, Canadian Boating Federation to Bill Braden, 26 August 1958

(18) Bill Braden Jr interview with the Author, 30 September 2009.

(19) <u>Ibid.</u>

(20) <u>Ibid.</u>

(21) <u>Ibid.</u>

(22) <u>Ibid.</u>

(23) <u>Ibid.</u>

(24) Bob Hutcheson interview with the author, 24 October 2009.

Mr. Hutcheson also recounted how Mrs. Braden said to him: "I've lived with this a few days" (as in 'I've been expecting this to happen at some time or other').

(25) <u>Ibid.</u>

(26) Bill Braden Jr Interview with the Author, <u>op. cit.</u>

In an interview with the author on 17 October 2009, Norm Braden recounts seeing his grandparents coming across the croquet area of the front lawn as the car pulled up and Francis Farwell saying: "I tried to tell him but he would not listen. I threatened him with 'he could not work for me if he continued on' but it did not work". He remembered his grandmother saying nothing, so overwhelmed was she for the loss suffered by her daughter and grandchildren.

(27) <u>Ibid.</u>

(28) <u>Ibid.</u>

(29) <u>Ibid.</u>

Bibliography

a) Primary Sources

Bill Braden Papers

Hamilton Street Railway Papers

Jim Thompson Papers

Library and Archives Canada Papers

b) Secondary Sources

"Braden-McColl", <u>Hamilton Spectator</u>, 4 December 1939.

<u>Echo de Rosey</u>, 1934.

<u>Hamilton City Directory</u>, 1910.

<u>Hamilton City Directory</u>, 1916.

<u>Hamilton City Directory</u>, 1924.

Ramsey, Winston G. (ed.) <u>The Blitz: Then and Now-Volume 3</u>. London: Battle of Britain Prints International Limited, 1990.

<u>The Globe and Mail</u>, 4 December 1939.

The Boar, #19, January 1952.

The Boar, #20, January 1953.

The Boar, #21, February 1954.

Trinity College School Record, December 1958.

Wansborough, Barry. Echoes That Remain. Hamilton: Hillfield-Strathallan College, 2001.

c) Interviews

Bill Braden
John Braden
Norm Braden
Gwyn Braden
Dave Braden
Harcourt Bull
Dorelle Cameron
Frank Cooke
Bob Hutcheson
Betty Leggett
Veronica Mallon
Ruby Moore
Russ Schleeh
Jim Thompson
'Sis' Wigle

d) Personal Correspondence

Viola Lyons
Carla Pruden
John Russo
Cindy Slinn
Barbara Stromstad